How and Where to Locate the Merchandise to Sell on eBay

Insider Information You Need to Know From the Experts Who Do It Every Day

Revised 2nd Edition

Zachary Humphrey and Alexander L. Kaplan, P.A.

HOW AND WHERE TO LOCATE THE MERCHANDISE TO SELL ON EBAY: INSIDER INFORMATION YOU NEED TO KNOW FROM THE EXPERTS WHO DO IT EVERY DAY — REVISED 2ND EDITION

Copyright © 2016 Atlantic Publishing Group, Inc.
1405 SW 6th Avenue • Ocala, Florida 34471 • Phone 800-814-1132 • Fax 352-622-1875
Web site: www.atlantic-pub.com • E-mail: sales@atlantic-pub.com
SAN Number: 268-1250

Library of Congress Cataloging-in-Publication Data

Humphrey, Zachary, 1992-
   How and where to locate the merchandise to sell on eBay : insider information you need to know from the experts who do it every day / by Zachary Humphrey and Alexander L. Kaplan, P.A. -- Revised 2nd edition.
      pages cm
   Revised edition of: How and where to locate the merchandise to sell on eBay / Michael P. Lujanac & Dan W. Blacharski. Ocala, Fla. : Atlantic Pub. Group, c2007.
   Includes bibliographical references and index.
   ISBN 978-1-60138-945-9 (alk. paper) -- ISBN 1-60138-945-0 (alk. paper) 1. eBay (Firm) 2. Internet auctions. 3. Purchasing. I. Kaplan, Alexander L. II. Lujanac, Michael P., 1955- How and where to locate the merchandise to sell on eBay. III. Title.
   HF5478.L85 2015
   658.8'777--dc23
                                        2015002220

Printed on Recycled Paper

Printed in the United States

Reduce. Reuse.
RECYCLE.

A decade ago, Atlantic Publishing signed the Green Press Initiative. These guidelines promote environmentally friendly practices, such as using recycled stock and vegetable-based inks, avoiding waste, choosing energy-efficient resources, and promoting a no-pulping policy. We now use 100-percent recycled stock on all our books. The results: in one year, switching to post-consumer recycled stock saved 24 mature trees, 5,000 gallons of water, the equivalent of the total energy used for one home in a year, and the equivalent of the greenhouse gases from one car driven for a year.

Over the years, we have adopted a number of dogs from rescues and shelters. First there was Bear and after he passed, Ginger and Scout. Now, we have Kira, another rescue. They have brought immense joy and love into not just into our lives, but into the lives of all who met them.

We want you to know a portion of the profits of this book will be donated in Bear, Ginger and Scout's memory to local animal shelters, parks, conservation organizations, and other individuals and nonprofit organizations in need of assistance.

– Douglas & Sherri Brown,
President & Vice-President of Atlantic Publishing

Disclaimer

The material in this book is provided for informational purposes and as a general guide to finding online merchandise for online businesses using eBay or other online auction sites. Atlantic Publishing does not guarantee success and is not liable for any money lost in pursuing an online venture using eBay or any other such marketing platform.

Table of Contents

Chapter 3: Now Cast a Wider Net......................59

Chapter 4: Becoming a Consignment Shop......79

Chapter 5: Pros and Cons of Using a Drop Shipper 83

Chapter 6: B2B, Liquidations, and Dedicated Manufacturers 97

Chapter 7: Buying Closeout Merchandise 101

Chapter 8: Wholesale Misconceptions 107

Chapter 9: Too Much Is Never Enough 115

Chapter 10: Finding Your Niche – Begin at the End... 125

Chapter 11: Your Strategy 137

Chapter 12: Finding and Selling Limited-Life Goods.. 141

Chapter 17: Building Business Relationships 203

Conclusion 211

Merchandise Directory 215

Introduction to the Second Edition

Why eBay?

EBay bills itself as Your Personal Trading Community™ and hosts well over 1 million online auctions per day in over a thousand categories. Every day the site gets about 3.5 million hits resulting in an average of $86 million changing hands. In addition, almost 150 million active eBay members create a frantic competition for the fortunes awaiting anyone willing to sit at a computer and earn some money.

Why is eBay so attractive to entrepreneurs? Is it the lure of easy money? It is true that eBay can provide a second income or bloom into a full-time business.

Is it the idea of being your own boss? Studies have shown that the highest levels of life's stress occur at work. (Even bosses would like to be their own boss.)

Is it the freedom from the 9 to 5 routine? Who would not want to set their own hours and goals with an eBay business? Who would not want to have their business on a computer they already own, avoid the time clock, work when, where and as much as they choose?

Is it because people already have the skills? Anyone – even you - can start a business this afternoon without going to school, getting special training, or even combing your hair.

Is it because there is very little risk? Your first salable products may actually be within your reach at this moment, or in the attic or in a closet, already bought and paid for. Where do you find other things to sell and make a profit? That is what this book is about. Read on.

Is it because the marketplace is huge? Your market is literally the world.

Is it because you can deal with products you know and love? If you love what you sell, online auctions are more than profitable. They are exciting.

By the time you finish this book you will have hundreds of tips for making money on this booming resource and having fun at the same time.

Are you limited to eBay? Certainly not. In the past few years, numerous other auction and retail sites have opened on the web, you just have to explore all the possibilities and gather all the information you can, including reports from other sellers as to their experiences on these other sales sites. What you do to prepare to sell on eBay translates into potential sales on more specialized sites. In recent years specialized sales sites have opened in all types of collectibles such as stamps, coins, antiques, firearms, military items, etc. Since eBay does not allow sales of some of these things, it is up to you to find your market for your specialized collectibles. In fact, because of numerous changes in the way eBay does business in the past few years, many of these alternate sales sites have become more attractive to sellers (and buyers) than eBay. More details about this development are featured later on in this book. The point is that what you learn in this book about selling on eBay generally applies to other web sales sites as well, only the finer details may be different.

Staying Power

Your choice of product is especially important if you want staying power on online auctions. We will explore in depth the art of finding the perfect products to sell in this book. A more important question at this point, however, is "How do I establish my products on eBay for the long-term?"

We have found that the most successful online auction sellers understand that making money on eBay is achieved the same way as success in a brick and mortar business, building from the bottom up. Like any smart sellers, you:

- Research the marketplace and the competition to determine the salability and profitability of the product. You can accomplish this on your computer without even getting dressed. Look at eBay's completed listings, compare the selling price to your buying price and related costs, and project your profits.

- Test the market with one or two items before committing to a product line and tying up cash. For right now, keep it safe and keep it simple.

- Adjust product offerings until you find a product or product line that sells consistently while you constantly research new possibilities for long-term income.

- Sell quality items. If your product does not hold up, you will be off eBay faster than a local store that sells sorry merchandise.

Why is your choice of product so important? For the private citizen, selling a product on eBay is not the same as selling that product at a flea market, farmers market, or small shop, primarily because of the extreme nature of the competition. When you go to the flea market to set up a weekend booth, you might have 100 other vendors competing for that dollar. Out of that 100, maybe two or three have the same things you do. On eBay, you may have thousands of competitors selling the same things you do. That is great for the buyer, but what will make your product better than others that are similar?

The answer is in having a better price, better quality, no-questions-asked return policy, realistic mailing costs, excellent customer service (fast replies to emails and questions), truth in advertising that establishes trust and assures return customers, detailed descriptions, anecdotes about the items that will make the owner proud, or the fact that you know your product better than most people. This book helps you find items that sell on eBay and tackles honing your skills as an online seller.

The thing to remember about selling on eBay is that, except in rare cases, it is not a get-rich-quick scheme. Like almost any type of successful business, it takes time to build, but you can build a profitable business just by selling on eBay. You can turn your eBay business into a profitable secondary income stream or even your primary income. All it takes is a little bit of work, good research, time, and effort, an eye for the unusual, and good customer service – and you will be rewarded. If you just want to sell a few items to make a little extra money, or if you want to sell many items and make a living selling on eBay, this book can help you do just that. Using the sources and ideas provided here, you will be able to find good products that will sell on eBay.

When you are searching for your goods to sell through eBay auctions or in your eBay store, there is more to it than going through a directory. Although we do include a directory in the back of this book, finding a good-selling product is only half the battle. You will need to establish your particular niche in the market for that product. We will go into niche marketing in detail. But for now, consider this:

Making a small margin on something that sells for more than $500 is fine, but let's say you are selling a $50 item and are only making 10 percent after expenses. You have to sell many items to make $500 a week. If you are selling anything for under $100, you will want to make a 25 percent net margin after cost, shipping, and eBay and PayPal fees.

Why Research?

We will explore research you will be doing to determine whether an item will be profitable. The best place to do your research is on eBay itself. This example illustrates the importance of checking out any given item on eBay before listing. Suppose you want to sell charm bracelets. They are popular and trendy, and local shops sell them well at a good profit. If you are selling them in your shop or at a local festival, you will do very well. However, as of this writing, there are almost 22,980 listings on eBay just for charms and charm bracelets, so chances are your own listing will not even get noticed. If it does, your competition will be so stiff that your profit margin will be negligible. If you bought 100 of them to get a bulk price, sell maybe two or three, you will have only gifts for friends and relatives. Obviously, another item will work better for you.

In the area of collectibles, you must research your product, thoroughly and preferably before you buy them in any quantity. Glass and glassware, pottery, stamps, coins, collectibles of all types, antiques in all its myriad areas (collectible jewelry, paintings, prints, old books), and anything else you can think of are specialized areas which require a great deal of advance knowledge to know what will sell and what is simply and truly trash from the perspective of the average consumer. It is important that you stick to your strengths. If you are a collector or a picker, sell what you know. Then go out and research other types of collectibles before you invest your hard-earned cash in what you are not as knowledgeable about. Remember the very first principal of picking: Just because it's old does not mean it's valuable. You have to know your product as well as know your market before you buy.

Be Ready to Switch Products

"When defeat comes, accept it as a signal that your plans are not sound, rebuild those plans, and set sail once more toward your coveted goal." — Napolean Hill

Finding good products means constantly being on the alert. Having a variety of goods listed on eBay will determine whether you make a little cash for a few weeks or have an income for the rest of your life, and the search will be a big part of your eBay business for as long as you are involved. Find a great product that no one else is selling but do not stop there. Keep on doing it, again and again.

Once you find an item that makes money, you will need to go against conventional wisdom and continue to search for other items. Flexibility is the key to success on eBay, since other merchants will be quick to spot something that is selling. Interest in that great item you have been getting 100 percent markup on may wane or others may get in on the action and decrease your margins. Staying with only one or two items may work in the short-term, but expect the demand to diminish and be prepared to get an updated version of your product or switch products altogether.

To see what is hot and what is not, what is rare, what you can buy low and sell high, all you need to do is surf eBay, look around the mega stores in your area, check out some online venues, and talk to your friends and their children. You never know how you will come across the next big thing or your next big thing, and when you do, you want to be the first to put it on eBay. You can sell small items in lots – beading supplies or toy cars – or the pricey pieces – expensive jewelry or a real car. You can appeal to people like yourself with whom you can establish an instant connection and trust, or you can apply your knowledge of a particular genre, your hobby, for instance, to draw a steady stream of customers. Whatever approach you take, this book will help you widen your sphere of sources.

What You Cannot Sell

Before we go any further, there are some things you are prohibited from listing on eBay. In a worst case scenario, trying to sell the items listed below can land you in legal trouble.

Items prohibited on eBay:

1. **Bootlegs** - Whatever you sell on eBay has to be original. Examples of bootlegs are copyrighted movie footage and rare music CDs. The United States cannot realistically control large-scale production in other countries, but sale or re-sale in the United States is still illegal.

2. **Copies** - Copies of computer software, particularly games, are available from overseas markets and black markets.

3. **Replicas** - Consider knock-off Gucci® handbags or RayBan® sunglasses replicas. Although they are often sold openly in stores in the United States, they are forbidden for sale on eBay.

4. **Copyrighted material** - Many people even steal copyrighted material from other sellers. Do not try selling it on eBay.

5. **Alcohol** - Prohibited on eBay.

6. **Smoking materials** - eBay does not allow sales of

cigarettes or any kind of tobacco products because their use is injurious to health.

7. **Firearms** - Weapons are regulated by U.S. law and cannot be sold on eBay. Even if you have a Federal Firearms License, which is required by the U.S. Government to deal in and ship modern firearms, eBay will not allow you to sell on the site. However, don't despair…there are numerous web sites where legitimate, licensed firearms dealers can sell their modern guns and accessories, along with military collectibles that eBay will not allow to be sold.

8. **De-scramblers** - Satellite and cable TV de-scramblers enable theft of service and cannot be sold at eBay.

9. **Animal Products** - eBay does not allow offering any product made from endangered animals or their skins.

10. **Tickets** - Some state laws prohibit scalping tickets; hence, they cannot be sold on eBay.

11. **Catalogs** - The only catalogs that can be sold on eBay are those dealing with collectible items.

12. **Prizes** - Putting up prizes for sale on eBay is prohibited.

13. Most military collectibles if they deal with or are related to modern weaponry such as weapon parts, simulators, etc. (see 7 above).

14. Anything else that eBay determines to be objectionable.

WARNING: This list is NOT all-inclusive. EBay is constantly changing what it allows and doesn't allow. The responsibility is yours to make sure you don't run afoul of eBay regulations. EBay does maintain beginner's pages and instructions on the site so that you can quickly determine what is permitted and what is not. If you have any questions, simply ask eBay before you list. This can be done online. Remember that if you intentionally list items that are prohibited, they will be pulled off by eBay. If you list disallowed items in a manner that seems more than accidental, your trading privileges can be suspended or revoked by eBay; after all, it is their website and ultimate control remains with them.

In the past, eBay has maintained review panels of knowledgeable people to review questioned listings such as stamps and coins for counterfeits, altered items (to make them more valuable than they actually are), etc. Recently, in an economic move and without any warning, eBay suspended the stamp and coin review panels. This opens up the marketplace to fraudulent sales. The one thing that can ruin your hard earned reputation on eBay as a reputable seller is a claim of fraud or counterfeiting. It is up to you to keep your reputation intact; know your own merchandise and make no claim about your merchandise in your listing unless you are sure it is true. It will help if you offer a no-questions-asked, money-back guarantee to your buyers on collectibles and such.

The U.S. Postal Service recommends that with all Internet transactions, you protect yourself and your family by following these tips:

- Check out all offers before making a decision. Check the seller's feedback and numbers of sales.

- Get all information in writing. Print out and keep all information on what you buy and sell.

- Do not give personal information to people or companies you do not know. For more information on fraud schemes, go to **https://postalinspectors.uspis.gov**.

Now you can buy and sell with some assurance of staying on legal ground and making money.

By the time you finish this book you will have hundreds of tips for making your money and having fun at the same time.

Chapter 1

Before You Sell Anything

Basic Steps in Selling on eBay

1. Read all the info that eBay provides explaining its process and the costs. EBay charges a listing fee that depends on the minimum price you will accept as well as a 10 percent commission when the item sells. If you list less than 50 items a month, there is no listing fee and you only pay a 10 percent commission to eBay when the item sells. If you are listing more than 50 items a month, you can look into becoming an "eBay Store," eBay Stores can list up to 2,500 items per month for free and then pay a discounted fee when an item sells. There is a monthly fee to eBay

for this; see the payments and fees regulations of eBay for further details and current pricing. Note that eBay's terms and conditions periodically change. You should review pricing and policies periodically so you don't get surprised when something changes.

2. Determine if you are listing the item as a "Buy it now" sale item or as an auction. The processes are different. When you sell by "Buy it now" you are selling at a fixed price just as if you were selling your goods in a brick-and-mortar store. You can also specify you will accept "best offers" if your "Buy it now" price is not met. An auction is just that, you agree to sell to the highest bidder. Don't panic, you can set a minimum sales price (a "reserve"). If the reserve is not met there is no sale. There is an additional fee for this, but when selling a high-priced item it protects the seller from losing out if

the reserve is not met. If you have questions about the fee structures, ask eBay before you make a costly mistake.

3. List your item, using good photos and a great deal of description. Make it clear if the buyer will pay for shipping and indicate the amount. If you have more than one similar item, write in each of your descriptions that you would be willing to consolidate shipments to save shipping costs (unless you are offering free shipping). You can also offer combined shipping on dissimilar sales if you desire. This can be attractive to buyers too.

4. When an item sells, you and the buyer contact each other by email and arrange for payment and shipment. EBay will generate an automatic invoice to your buyer and email it for you. EBay then charges your account a percentage of the final sale price. If your item doesn't sell the first time, you can often relist it for free (if it sells the second time eBay refunds the listing fee). This only applies to auction sales, not "Buy it now" sale items.

5. EBay now insists on the use of PayPal for payment on most, if not all items. This means that you must open a PayPal account and tie it to a credit card or bank account as well as to your eBay account. There are fees involved when you receive or make payments through PayPal too, so you must read and understand how PayPal works as well as eBay. EBay purchased PayPal in 2002. Since that happened, eBay has prohibited payment with credit cards, checks, money orders, etc. From one point of view that is good for buyers and sellers, it provides a degree

of security in the financial end of the transaction. On the other hand, it becomes monopolistic and another means for eBay to make money off the buyer and seller in addition to the fees for the listing and sale. A PayPal account, however, can be used outside of the eBay environment. Many online businesses accept PayPal; we have even seen some commercial brick-and-mortar stores accepting PayPal. Other auction sites may offer PayPal too, but usually accept payment by checks, credit cards, money orders, etc. Again, read the terms and conditions of each auction site.

6. After delivery of the goods, the buyer writes feedback on the transaction on eBay, which serves as a reference for future buyers who want to find out how well you do business. Timely shipping is a key here; sellers must also carefully follow eBay instructions regarding insurance, tracking, delivery, etc. in order to receive "seller protection" in the event that a sale goes bad.

7. When you first post items for sale, a sunglasses ("shades") icon appears next to your name. That symbol indicates that you are either a newcomer or you have changed your online name recently, perhaps because of a bad reputation from a previous identity. "Shades" are a warning sign, indicating "Buyer beware. Nothing is known about this seller." That symbol lasts for a month.

Then you get a gold star, and, if you have good feedback, you are on your way. Your feedback is your reputation. Read the eBay instructions carefully so that you fully understand how feedback works. Know too that it is very hard to remove bad feedback from your account, even if you really did nothing wrong at all and just had problems with a nasty buyer. If you get more than three bad feedbacks in a short period of time, eBay can temporarily suspend or even, in worse cases, permanently prohibit you from future participation as an eBay seller or buyer.

A good title for your listing, a detailed description of your item and clear photographs are also keys to successful sales.

In most cases, buyers will enter a key word to search for items of interest. A good title can be critical for buyers to find your item, so make the title as descriptive and specific as you possibly can. Before you list, look at other items for sale similar to yours. Try and see which items are getting the most bids and attention and be guided by the title of those sales when creating your own. Plagiarism here is NOT a problem, but a misleading or inaccurate title may result in no sale. This doesn't mean you can copy another seller's listing wholesale and use it for yourself, be creative, make it your own before you copy another's work.

Description is also extremely important. Be as specific as you can be. State if it's new or used; any damage, missing parts, etc. that you know of. Honesty is the best policy. If you say there is a fault in an item, a disgruntled buyer will not have grounds to reverse the sale if you clearly described the fault the buyer is complaining of, "Caveat Emptor" (let the buyer beware). State whether the item works or not (if this applies). List anything that may help the sale. Remember too that a buyer can search for items not only by the title but by keywords in your description, so don't be sparing on how you word your sale. A few extra descriptive words in your listing can mean the difference between a particular buyer finding your listing or not.

Photographs can make or break your sales. Clear detailed digital photographs can show a buyer what he/she would be able to see if he/she could handle the item at a yard sale or show it in a store. Show any damages or irregularities in the photos, in addition to the good stuff. Again, let the buyer beware. If you are just getting started and don't own one, borrow a friend's decent quality digital camera and experiment with lighting, background, exposure, etc., until you are comfortable with using the photos to represent your product.

Look at photos of other sellers to see what works and what doesn't. Sooner or later you will need to purchase a camera for yourself, so get the best quality digital camera you can afford. You'll make up the cost in no time if you take good photos for your listings. Another option is to utilize the camera application on your smart phone as several phones offer the potential of photo capture that often rivals most affordable cameras in terms of quality. Remember that with many collectibles, condition can mean the difference between a 25 cent sale and a $50 sale. This is especially true with items whose values are directly related to their usability, such as stamps and coins. Close-up photos are thus critical in determining and showing condition. Some dealers will have 10, 20 or even more photos of each item being sold to demonstrate the true condition of the item to potential buyers, though very simple items will require less photos than their complex counterparts.

Research for Profitability

One of the most critical tasks to undertake before investing in a quantity of goods to sell on eBay is that you determine whether you can make a profit on your purchases. Besides simply finding out who sells what, which we will cover later, you also have to research whether the product will sell. The process of selling merely allows you to realize that profit. In other words, you really need to make informed buying decisions. This is accomplished with solid product research. Know what is going to sell so you do not end up with a truckload of last year's fad that no one wants.

Only buy something to resell on eBay after you have thoroughly researched that particular product, the market, and the competition. Make sure the item will sell at a profit. One good site that helps with research is **www.HammerTap.com** from Bright Builders. You even get a trial run that is free for the first 10 days.

You need to be familiar with pricing and demand for the product. Where do you find this information? EBay is a great repository of useful data. The challenge here is how to translate it into usable information for yourself. This is where the experience you developed from selling your own items will come in handy. Once you become familiar with all the details of eBay, your do not need a marketing degree to make a good determination of what will sell and how much markup you can expect.

Every successful entrepreneur has done his or her "due diligence" which just means research: doing your homework.

> Researching on eBay is critical to learning the value any item has on eBay. It pays to know your market and understand your product mix before you go shopping for items to sell.

Sell-through Rate

The sell-through rate is something many eBay merchants ignore to their detriment. When doing your cost calculations, naturally you figure in how much your eBay listing fees are going to be, but if only one in 10 of your items actually sells, that calculation gets thrown off substantially.

For example, suppose your eBay listing fees are $1.50 and you are hoping to get $10 per item for something that cost you $5. With 15 percent going for fees and 50 percent going for cost, that is 65 percent, leaving you a 35 percent profit. But do not stop the calculations there. Suppose though, that only one in ten of your items sells. For every ten items, now you have paid $15 in fees, and spent $50 on inventory, for a total of $65 in cost, for a return of only $10. Now you have lost money.

The lesson here is that before you start counting your profits, take a very close look at the product category on eBay to determine how many are actually being sold and how many are getting no bids at all. These lessons are what separate you from a one-time seller to someone who runs a legitimate eBay business for profit.

You can do your own research or use one of several available software tools to do this type of market research for you. An example is eBay Profit Calculator at **http://salecalc.com**.

Regardless of what you sell, do not expect everything to have a 100 percent sell-through rate. It is just not going to happen, not on eBay and not anywhere else. That is why you see all those great overstock sales all the time. If a particular item category has a sell-through rate of 35 percent or higher, you can do very well with it if you price it right.

Think Globally, Act Locally

Obtain locally. Sell globally. EBay is better than local venues for selling most items, especially when you have something that

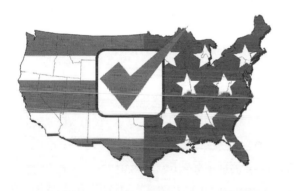

has a high value. You might think that buying something to sell is the first thing to do, but let us back up first for a second. We are going to share with you the same sources we have frequently employed to locate items to sell on eBay. There are unlimited places you can look to find products to sell, but if you are new to online auctions, the best place to start is right in the place where you live, so hang onto your money for now.

You must remember that selling globally can create its own problems and difficulties. Customs regulations, shipping costs and time in transit all have an affect on your ability to sell globally. Some countries prohibit the importation of certain items like jewelry, valuable metals, military items, etc. As seller, it is up to you to know what you can sell and what you cannot in a given country. If you are just starting out on eBay, you might want to limit your sales to just the United States and perhaps Canada, at least until you feel comfortable with the operation and have time to do the research needed. Fraud is a major problem when dealing with overseas sales, so always keep that in mind as well.

Start slowly by finding a few things around your home that you no longer need and list them on eBay. It is vitally important that a potential seller understand the process before investing any money in a quantity of product. You need to get some eBay selling experience. Just playing with eBay a bit before you go into it in a big way will give you a good "feel" for how it works.

My experience began with selling whatever came my way, then moving to a more traditional reselling model where I chose which products I want to sell. Originally, I was a consignment seller, and then a certified Trading Assistant. Finding products meant finding clients. When I did not have clients, I haunted garage sales, thrift stores, auctions, and rummage sales. However, over time, I began selling more traditional commodity-type items.

> The "one item/one listing" model many eBay merchants use when starting out is too labor intensive for an ongoing business. I prefer to buy a case lot and write just one description that I can post over and over. Writing one listing that can be used 12 times frees me up to take care of other parts of my business.

When you have finished selling items from your house, it is time to start acquiring items at garage sales and thrift shops. As they sell (or not), you will see patterns emerging – those items that sell well and those that are easy to buy. Perhaps you will find your place in the market is one that no one else occupies. A friend of mine found that rug crafters would buy any item made of wool, dye it, and artfully weave it into items to sell on eBay. He now has a steady eBay business supplying used woolen blankets and garments to rug hobbyists.

By looking only casually, you will find artists and craftspeople, small manufacturers, distributors, and, of course, plenty of ordinary people with old stuff collecting dust in their attics. You will be surprised at how much you can find to sell at a profit within a few miles of your home.

Old crockery, pieces of china, clothing (in good condition), unwanted gift items, duplicate items, old watches, crystal glass, costume jewelry. Search any place where you or your relatives or friends store old items. Few people would mind having someone clear out junk from their house. What is junk to them can jumpstart your career on eBay.

After scouring those venues, try going to yard sales, local auctioneers' businesses, estate sales, thrift and consignment stores, and church bazaars. Local venues can be terrific places to buy things to sell on eBay. They can be better than a gold mine. When you graduate from them, you can branch out and find national distributors, liquidators, drop shippers, and wholesalers, and trading associates. We will examine each of these sources. Just remember, the world is waiting to buy what you find locally.

Also, as the world becomes ever more connected through technology, don't forget the opportunities available through social media. Facebook offers a great, free space in which to connect both potential buyers and sellers together. For example, there are often local groups on Facebook that serve as a makeshift online community in which small business owners can communicate with one another about buying and selling their wares individually as well as in group events, such as green markets, annual events such as Small Business Saturday, the holiday between Black Friday and Cyber Monday. Often tired by faceless, commercial giants, many consumers are turning to small businesses to attain good quality products with a person they can legitimately interact with. Knowing which angle to push is often half the battle.

Just keep in mind what we said earlier…when dealing with collectibles, antiques, art, etc., you must have some basic knowledge about what you are buying so that you do not overpay for the item; after all, you're doing this to make some money…not lose it by overpaying. Remember too that just because something is old, it does NOT mean it is worth more, someone else must see the value in it and be willing to buy it, otherwise it is just old trash.

Find Out What People Are Buying on eBay Today

Whatever it is, it may be different tomorrow. Trends or fads have a double bell curve in profitability: selling high as they catch on with the public, then low as interest wanes, and high again as they become rare. This is especially true when dealing with antiques, collectibles, etc. In recent years there has been a wild fluctuation in such markets. You must know your market before you buy in order to sell at a profit.

If you know what stage the trend is in at this moment with any given product, you can then easily predict its profitability. Spend some time just becoming familiar with eBay. Surf through the pages and the different categories and try to take notice of the actual number of items getting bids in each category. Spend some time visiting the many eBay forums, and you will be able to gain even more information as to what is hot and what is not. One thing to know is that while eBay is a friendly community, vendors can be tight-lipped about their success strategies. If they have a hot product they are making money on, it is not likely they will share their source with you.

If you are considering acquiring a product to resell, take a look on eBay, and see how many other similar products are on offer. If there are too few, it may be because there is no demand. If there are too many, there may be too much competition, and your listing will get lost. Look at the eBay Keyword page, which will show you some of the most popular search terms that people have entered into the eBay search engine. It is a little difficult to read, but it is very valuable information that you should get to know. Alternately, click on the "Seller Central" page and go to the "What is Hot" section, and you can get a very good idea there of what is popular. The "Hot Items by Category" button will yield a lengthy PDF report that is reliable.

Of course, one of the best ways to discover what is selling on eBay is to play the role of the buyer. Even if you do not actually buy anything, spend some time watching auctions. Watch carefully how the bidding goes and notice how many bidders that different types of items attract. Look into auctions that have already closed to see what has gone without bids and what garnered a high price.

Chapter 2

Where to Begin Looking for a Product

Start where you live

Many local communities have a web board or online bulletin board, such as **www.Ocala4Sale.com** in Ocala, Florida. Other sites, such as **www.buymystuff.com** and **www.Craigslist.net**, are nationally known and used throughout the United States from Alaska to Florida, but they are categorized into several local sections so that you can mine these sites for great products near you.

I personally have had great experiences with Ocala4Sale specifi-cally, and you can have just as much success with similar sites that target your local area. Although I have had success answer-ing specific ads, sometimes a listing may lead to something com-pletely unexpected. Most recently, I was surfing through this site and noticed a yard sale listing that advertised DVDs and CDs in Crystal River, Florida. I drove there and found the address, but there was no yard sale going on.

Next door, however, was a little strip mall, and I decided to check out the businesses there. After all, I had just driv-en 40 miles, and if there were anything of merit in the strip mall, at least the trip would not be a total loss. One of the storefronts was the Florida Sheriff's Youth Ranch Thrift Store. They had the usual thrift store junk but also a very nice selection of non-fiction books, with paperbacks selling for 25 cents and hard covers for 50 cents. I selected a shopping cart full of non-fiction books in like new condition and sold them for ten times their cost.

Local Storage Companies

If your city or town has any "you-store-it" type of businesses, give them a call to see if they have regular auctions on any aban-doned property. Most "you-store-it" companies have at least an occasional customer who did not pay the rent or never returned to claim their items after the rental term was complete. In this case, the storage unit's owners have to abide by laws that require them to attempt to locate the owner, but after all attempts have failed, they may dispose of the stored items to recoup lost rent or to clear up the space for other renters.

You may or may not get to look at the actual items stored, and you may have to purchase the entire lot to win the auction, but it is a chance that can really pay off. You will be right to assume that if a person took the time to store items, there is something of value among them. Even if most of the contents have little resale value, it may only take a few items to make the deal lucrative for you.

Be sure to determine the conditions of the auction before you go. Most storage auctions require a cash payment on the spot. Some may accept credit cards or checks, but this is sketchy, so make sure you know the requirements before you go. Know too if you have to empty the storage bay out the same day or do they give you a day or so to get this done. Disposing of any trash or unwanted stuff from the storage bay is your job; you can't take what you want and leave the rest. Don't expect the storage place to allow you to use their dumpster for trash either, so come prepared to do what is needed and know in advance where to take the trash.

Flea Markets

As one who has sold at flea markets, I can safely say that this type of venue is a buyer's market not a seller's market. People tend to come to most flea markets in search of a bargain, and treat it as a sort of large, extended yard sale. It does not matter what you are selling there; people will always try to buy it for less. If I had a basket of dollar bills in a flea market booth and tried selling them two for a dollar, people would still try to bargain with me.

While selling at the flea market is often a frustrating experience, especially if you have quality goods, going there to shop can be rewarding. If vendors have had a really bad day because the weather was too bad or too good for people to shop, they may not have even made enough to cover their booth rent and will do anything for a sale. Find out what they have, tell them what you are looking for, and you will be surprised at the deals you can make.

Flea markets can be useful to get rid of the lesser-valued stuff that isn't worth selling online. After a few months of hunting goodies, you'll probably find you have a lot of excess stuff that isn't worth the trouble of selling on eBay or another auction site. That's where selling at a flea market comes in.

Veteran successful flea marketers are often pack rats and will usually have a garage jammed full of all sorts of items. They may not even know what is in there, and more often than not, what they have on display at the flea market is only a small percentage of their stock. Tell them what you are interested in, and you have a good chance of hearing, "Oh yeah, I have a box full of those in my garage." You may pick up that box for a fraction of the amount you will get on resale.

The flea market has an eclectic mix of trash and treasure, and anything can be the start of your new business. Be aware that worthless items outnumber treasures, but once you go on the hunt, chances are you will not go home empty-handed. You may just get lucky and find that special item in the 50-cent bin that you can turn around and resell for a $1,000.

Once again, knowing your merchandise is critical to turning a profit. There isn't much point in arguing a seller down to $10 for a piece of Depression glass that you won't be able to sell on eBay for more than $5 because there are hundreds of identical pieces of glass online. If you are looking for jewelry, either costume or precious, always carry a jeweler's loupe or similar magnifier. Looking for maker's marks, jewelry markings of pureness or quality can be very difficult. A loupe is also useful when looking at stamps, coins, glassware and such to determine flaws, condition, etc. Get a 10X triplet magnifier (3 lenses in a case with 10 power magnification). These are useful for almost all examinations except looking for bacteria. A good quality triplet can be purchased for around $20. Again, condition is everything when it comes to antiques, collectibles, jewelry, etc.

Constantly explore eBay and the other auction sites you may deal with to see where the market is, what's selling and what's not, before you go hunting at flea markets. This will help you avoid what may be a costly mistake. You not only have to know how much to pay for something, but what you may get back on the resale.

Yard Sales

Of course, we would be remiss if we did not mention the ubiquitous yard sale, an American celebration of excess. You will find yard sale vendors of all different levels of sophistication and people who hold yard sales for many different reasons. While some people hold them just to get rid of unwanted junk – sometimes acquired at other yard sales, others hold them to raise

money and are out to earn as much as they can get. Similarly, some people holding yard sales know the value of what they have, and others do not. I have shopped at yard sales only occasionally since joining eBay, but I have found a set of vintage wood carders for $0.10 that are worth about $20 and a millefiori vase, marked $1, that normally sells for $350.

Yard sales are fabulous for picking up children's games – video, computer, and board– as they sell quickly on eBay. Just make sure in advance that they are complete and not missing parts or instructions. I have an energetic friend who has a full-time job, co-owns a weekend drink stand at a flea market, and derives a good, steady third income from selling games on eBay. His teens are as caught up in his constant round of work as he is and have eagerly taken over managing his eBay store and auctions. If you see a popular board game that is missing pieces and you can get it for $0.50, it might be worth your while to grab it and hold onto it until you can complete the game with parts from another sale… but remember that the ultimate goal is to make money from the exercise, so don't wind up paying $5 for a game you can only sell for $5…breaking even isn't the way to profitability.

I do not recommend straying far from your home base unless you are aware ahead of time that a particular item that you are knowledgeable about is being offered because the community yard sale is a favorite target of antique collectors, eBay sellers, and others, so you may find them a bit over shopped. Plus the popularity of eBay has drawn potential sellers away from holding yard sales. Nonetheless, you can still find some unusual items at yard sales.

I have found that yard sellers and marketers are there to sell their stuff and get rid of it quick. Therefore, I have approached many and asked them if I bought the majority of their goods, would they be willing to cut me a deal. I also find that by stopping in at the end of the day at yard sales and flea markets, you can get even a better deal at closing time as they want to "sell out" quick and go home. You will be delighted at the deals you can get using this method.

There is always some disagreement among serious yard sale shoppers as to the best time to shop. While some get up before dawn to be first in line before everything is picked through, others visit yard sales toward the end of the day to snap up bargains and make lot offers: "I will buy everything you have left for $25." Both strategies are valuable. Either arrive early for the one great buy before anyone else gets it, or arrive late to buy things the owner does not want to take back into the house such as books. Lifting an unwanted box of books is daunting after a day of selling. To your advantage, listing and mailing just one book can be profitable.

At any time of day, feel free to make an offer for everything in one or more categories, such as books, CDs, DVDs, and especially children's clothing. Any reasonable seller would rather sell many things at once at less than their total marked price than to sit for hours waiting for a dollar here and there.

When I go to yard sales, I use a trick I learned from my Dad. He collected and restored vintage autos before the Internet age. He would spend hours at swap meets looking for those special auto parts to complete his project. I loved to go with him, especially to see the twinkle in his eye when he found that long searched for part. One of his favorite tricks was to keep cash in different amounts in each pocket. That way he could pull out a few dollars and tell the dealer he only had that much, or he would pull out a roll of twenties and start counting when haggling over a higher value item. Ironically, when the dealers saw a wad of cash, they were more likely to come down in their prices. There is something magical about a roll of bills. If you enjoy haggling, you can sometimes reduce the asking price by 30 percent or more. It never hurts to try.

One word of caution, since inventories vary so much, do not expect to base your whole eBay business on yard sales. However, if you acquire items that prove to be unwanted by eBay buyers, you can usually recoup your investment at your own yard sale.

Church Community Sales

Churches often have annual or semi-annual community sales as fundraisers. Newspapers often carry listings of these events, and you can usually see them advertised on church signs as you drive by. The quality and quantity of goods at these regular events is often much higher than at yard sales, since church members and their friends are donating goods for the benefit of their religious organization rather than holding their individual yard sales or trying to sell on eBay. They have a greater motivation to put out quality items than anyone who just wants to clean out a garage or attic. This is the place to be at the end of the day.

After a long day of lifting, loading, selling, standing, rearranging, cooking, and socializing, volunteers are loath to pack up leftover goods and find places to store them until disposal. Offer to take the merchandise away for them or make an offer on a group of items that you believe to be worth something. After you have gone through your buys and culled out resalable items, drop the rest off at a charity thrift store and get a receipt for a tax deduction.

If you know what your market is in advance, you can make a nice profit on things you find at church and school community sales. A few years ago I went to a church sale and bought a box of old microphones for $10. I knew in advance that they were collectible; when I finished on eBay I had turned them over for an almost $200 profit, as well as keeping one for my own collection of antique radios and equipment.

Local Newspaper

Even your local newspaper can become a source of merchandise. Regularly scan classified listings or place an ad stating the type of used items you want to purchase. The "legal notices" section of your paper may clue you in to auctions of seized and abandoned property, and these can be valuable sources of highly salable goods.

Here, too, you want to look for "collections" that an heir may not appreciate. You may find someone selling off a collection of old photos, books, costume jewelry, antiques, stamps, coins, comics, rare baseball cards, or anything that someone inherited from a relative (or that a divorced spouse left behind – their "good bye" can mean your good buy!). Now the owner just wants them out of the house. Once again, and we can't keep saying it enough, you must have an idea of what you are buying before you shell out your hard-earned dollars…you must know you can turn a profit of what you buy, unless you just want it for your own collection.

Local Auctions

I used to attend an auction every month or so run by the local computer warehouse. I would also get impact printers for $1 or so. I got 30 to 40 times that on eBay because even though they were obsolete, some applications required them   such as carbon forms. I noticed that my credit union used the same model printer I had recently sold.

The pace of those particular auctions was excruciating, however, and many people just got bored and dropped out, to my advantage. I recommend that even if you can hardly hold your eyes open and you do not see anything worth buying for the first few hours, do not leave! Specific product auctions that you cannot rummage through ahead of time are full of surprises. You may sit through a couple of hours of nothing and then see a real gem of an item on the podium, pick it up for $25, and resell it later for $200.

While you may be able to make a deal with the auctioneer before or after the auction, your success may depend on just having patience to sit and wait it out. At this particularly excruciating auction, they would routinely hold up a PC mouse and drone on, "Do I hear a $1 for this mouse?" Thank heavens for caffeine! It was almost like work to sit through the mouse pads, keyboards, power cords, and the other mundane items one needed in the PC replacement part business, but it was still worth it.

As a computer warehouse and reseller, the owner had regular access to laptops. I would normally pay around $200 to $225 each, and resell on eBay for $300 to $375. Not a bad margin overall, and they made the few hours of boredom well worthwhile. Buying and selling computers has changed drastically since then in the specific details, but the lessons learned from these auctions still prove to be vital even today.

Don't overlook box lots at auctions; try and rummage through them in advance to see what's in each lot. I bought a box lot of electronics at a local auction, knowing that there was a valuable and collectible Volt-Ohm meter in the box from a railroad. I sold off the junk, got back what I paid for the box lot, and then sold the valuable meter on eBay for $150. That was pure profit for me. At church and school bazaars, if you see a box with stuff you want in it, don't be afraid to make an offer on the whole box; very often you'll pay much less for the whole box than if you started picking and choosing from the box in front of the sales people.

Thrift Shops

It is not surprising that a large percentage of the people who shop at places like Goodwill, the Salvation Army, and other charity thrift shops and donation centers are people who are looking for things to resell. Find out which day of the week the store is replenished from its stock of donations and get there early. You will recognize the pros. Ask them what they are looking for and offer to help them find it. You will learn a great deal.

After you visit these shops for a while, you will get to know which ones have the best goods. They vary tremendously. Some may have many low-quality, commodity-type goods. These are the shops where you can find a set of used dishes, a nice suit, or a second-hand couch, and they are great for college students or people who truly need the goods, but they are not likely to turn up the profitable resalable items.

However, do not get discouraged. You will find those thrift shops or consignment shops that carry a large selection of up-scale goods in excellent shape. You may very well find valuable antiques, paintings, and designer clothes that can be resold for many times your purchase price.

Recently, a friend bought a painting at the St. Vincent de Paul Society thrift shop for $5. She has an excellent artistic eye and recognized value when she saw it. It turned out to be worth more than $1,000.

Interestingly, clothing is one of the top-selling categories on eBay, and if you know what you are looking for, you may well be able to pick up a designer outfit or exquisite formal dress at a consignment shop for an extraordinary profit. (Or you may become the shop's eBay expert, sharing in the profits of everything you list for them. Check out the section in this book on "Trading Assistants.") Dealing in clothing on eBay takes a good eye for quality. If you know the best labels or have a good feel for what is trendy, you will find items that are good sellers. In recent years, vintage clothing from the 1950's through 1970's has become a very hot area for resale. Vintage clothing that has never been worn and has original tags still on is a gold mine for sellers of such merchandise.

Estate Sales

Estate sales are great places to find items that attract collectors on eBay: reel to reel tape recorders, old electric signs and displays advertising bygone merchandise, books, old hinges (artists and decorators are your customers), doorknobs, drawer pulls, and tools. Although you are competing with family members who, you would think, have scavenged for the best items, often relatives take only the things of no value that are sentimental to them and overlook familiar pieces that someone, somewhere, covets. EBay is the best place to find that "someone." One estate sale a week can become a good second income and a satisfying hobby. If an item fails on eBay – it is the item's fault, not yours, it can be sold from your home or to a brick and mortar antique store.

The one constant when trying to get inventory to sell is estate sales. These are not yard sales, but traditional sales and auctions, and the quality and quantity of goods is usually much more diverse and of higher quality. Sometimes auction houses buy entire contents of homes and run what they call "Attic, Barn, and Basement" sales. These events usually consist of household items that would not provide enough revenue for individual sale at an auction, but when combined with quantities of related items make a great way to acquire inventory. Some refer to these events as "table top" auctions.

When you go to them, you bid on the entire contents of a single table. Many of the items you get at these auctions are ultimately destined for Goodwill® or the Salvation Army®, but you can find items that people seek out on eBay. Even if you buy a table or a lot, give half of it away to Goodwill, and sell the rest on eBay, chances are you will still turn a good profit. Again, make sure to get a donation receipt so that you can take a tax deduction.

I make it a point not to spend too much on these tables and usually come away from an auction having spent maybe $40 to $50. My profits have reached as much as $800 to $1,000 per table on a really good one. I have always made money on these tables, not always a huge score, but it does happen.

I have been going to real time auctions for more than 40 years and I love them! I live in a rural area and there are auctions within 60 miles about every weekend. Most auctions are open for inspection a day or two before the auction date. If I am looking for something to sell on eBay, it is essential to visit the auction and do a complete walk through several times. If there are items that might bring bids on eBay, there is time to go home and research them before buying them. When I go into the auction, I know how much I am willing to spend for the day and for any given item I rarely go over my price. EBay and auctions are both competitive markets and it takes a little time to get a "feeling" for what will sell.

Be the Last in Line

You know they say the early bird gets the worm, but what about the "early worm?" Hit that rummage sale late as they are literally pulling up stakes. The day is waning and sellers are willing to agree to almost anything. Of course, the sharks have already picked off the good stuff (or so they think!) but how can $2,000 in premium merchandise (I paid $25 for a truckload) go untouched for two days? Answer: All that glitters is not gold   gold is often mistaken for sand.

I passed a church on my street that was having an outdoor rummage sale recently. There I found boxes of books   dozens of boxes, full of new hardcover non-fiction books and textbooks on such subjects as history, philosophy, and comparative religion. Most had a four-digit catalog number on the first page, and were otherwise in pristine condition. There were even valuable old first editions from someone's collection. The folks running the sale were closing up for the evening, and I picked out three boxes and paid $5 for each box. When I got home, I looked up a few of the books on **www.Bookfinder.com**, and discovered that most of them were worth $20 and $30 each.

I happily returned the next evening as they were pulling up stakes. While they were wearily tearing down the tent and packing it in, I asked how much for the rest of the books and was ready to pay $150 easily. They said $10 total, I said fine, and I filled the entire bed of my pickup with boxes of valuable books. When I listed them on eBay to resell them, I got $28.88 for just one book in that very first batch. I made my money back with just one sale, and still had a truckload of books left to sell at a fine profit.

A word of caution here, not all books are valuable or collectible. You have to explore the market in advance. Do NOT take your unsellable books to a used bookstore either; you are better to donate them to a charity thrift store. Most used bookstores won't pay more than a few cents for softcovers and rarely (unless it is really valuable) more than 50 cents for hardcovers. By donating them to a charity thrift store, you can deduct considerably more for them at tax time. Just make sure you make a list of each title and whether it's hardcover or softcover before you donate them and get a receipt from the charity for the donation. The IRS demands this; otherwise they may try and disallow your donation.

One thing on courtesy here, do not go to a sale and then start looking things up on your smart phone in front of the seller, this is downright rude. Walk away if you must do your research and then come back when you are ready to buy. At a recent garage sale when I was disposing of some unwanted things, one buyer kept looking everything up while standing in front of my table, effectively blocking other buyers from viewing and buying. I finally asked the buyer to step away to make room for others.

Go for the package price and volume discounts. Buy it all sometimes. Always make offers lower than you expect to pay and meet in the middle. Always let the sellers give you their best price first. Then you offer an even lower price.

If you are not sure of the marketability either from your knowledge of product or eBay research, it is best to pass up the item unless you want it for personal use. You might ask the seller for a telephone number so you can call later to offer a price (after checking for similar items on eBay).

Check the item carefully for condition. Broken or damaged items do not sell well on eBay.

Bottom line is:
   a. Make sure you can sell it before you buy it.
   b. Offer less than you are willing to pay and negotiate up.
   c. Offer to buy several items for a reduced price.
   d. Check item well for condition.

Far from the Maddening Crowd

Sometimes, peddling what is hot can be profitable, but the downside to that is there are already thousands of other people selling the same thing. Buyers know that there is so much competition with those "hot" items. Because of price pressure, the price will naturally sink. This is supply and demand.

From the seller's perspective, sometimes, what is hot is what is not what you want. Seek out the mundane item that will yield the numbers you want and avoid the hot item everyone else is hawking. Boring can be beautiful. I used to get $25 to $30 for an obscure tape drive. I had no idea what they were at first, so I went to eBay, input the model number in a search, and checked the little box indicating I wanted to search the main text as well as the headline, included past auctions, and sorted within those results by price, from high to low. I then borrowed from that text, altering it just enough to make it seem different, and kept the operative elements. A tape drive   how boring is that? Pretty boring. Of course, they came FREE with the already heavily discounted Dell PCs I needed anyway. Suddenly, they were providing a steady stream of income and were not so boring anymore! Both tape drives and Dell PCs are a thing of the past, but the lesson we can learn from this still persists: Boring can be very profitable.

The attractive element here is that items like the tape drive are not in great demand, but they are nonetheless very necessary to some people. This is not a collectible item. It is not necessarily an antique. It is just an ordinary commodity computer part that many people with old computers want. If you have a good source for these types of goods, you can make a steady profit on eBay with them.

Peter Lynch, manager of the Magellan Fund, at the time the world's largest mutual fund, wrote a book called *One Up on Wall Street*. In it, he detailed his preference for the mundane and the commonplace. His car of choice? Lynch drove an 11-year-old AMC Concord that was not yet completely rusted out. His favorite stocks included Crown Cork and Seal, makers of bottle caps. Bottle caps? How ordinary is that? I cannot think of anything more boring than bottle caps, but of course, every household in the consuming world had bottle caps at that time.

Another of his favorites was Service Corp International, the funeral home giant. How dull is that? Everyone dies though, so that makes getting paid more important than being trendy. Lynch did very well. Many times in the stock market and corporate world, the companies that make the flashy products do very well for a short time and burn out quickly, but it is the companies that make socks who have staying power.

Trendy things are great but they require keeping a pulse on American taste, which can easily change overnight. Go with the money, no matter how dull, uncool, or mundane it may seem. Your wisdom will always trump pop culture bad habits.

Facebook and Final Notes

There is not a specific location to buy goods through Facebook. This really comes through groups/friends who have items to sell and you can do so that way, by simply communicating with your friends or joining Facebook groups in your area. Also, based on your contacts and interests, ads may be sent to you via your Facebook page, but all dealings are ultimately with the company, not Facebook.

However, as an individual, you may join a local Freecycle website; apparently is it different in each community. You can buy books, toys, furniture, appliances, clothes, etc. Flea markets, trade shows, friends, family, and consignment shops are also recommended. Garage sales, going out of business sales, outlets and clearance stores. These are entirely valid options as well.

Some final sites that are highly recommended include: iOffer (a San Francisco-based online trading community), ePier (a no listing fee online auction site), Craig's List (the infamous online classified advertisements site), and finally Ubid (an excellent online auction style and fixed-price shopping website).

Chapter 3

Now Cast a Wider Net

*W*hen you are first getting started, finding your inventory locally is often the best way to go, as we saw in the previous chapter. But after a while, your business will grow, and you will want to look beyond your local area. Doing so will give you a wider selection of goods to choose from and a better chance of finding new, high quality, highly desirable items that you will not be able to find at your local flea market. Of course, when you broaden your resource initiatives, you can expect to find much better deals by buying in quantity and selling individual items.

It is better overall marketing to start small and build to quantity purchasing when you have:
1. established a market for the product.
2. built feedback on eBay and have established customers.

Start small; when considering large lots, ask for samples. As you develop good business relationships, compile a list of sources, wholesale and retail, drop shippers, dealers, websites, and sellers in your area. To get you started we have put a directory in this book. Your own list is worth money to other sellers! Later on, we will discuss selling information itself online.

Buying in large quantities saves on shipping costs. Test by buying small numbers, but if you find a great deal on quantity be willing to take a risk. Risk is how you get big payoffs. When selecting a supplier, look for reliability, a good track record, and good prices.

I do find it best to buy in larger quantities as I save a lot of money this way. Sometimes you will find yourself stuck with a few leftovers, but if you have an eBay store, store them there, or bundle and sell them in a large lot for wholesale prices. You can at least recoup your money.

For the most part, I buy in the largest quantity I can afford to get the best discount. However, in every store or retail business there are items that a seller must have on hand, even though they are slow movers.

If possible, I try to keep those types of items in inventory, but buy the fewest I can. That may mean a smaller profit, but if it keeps the customer coming back, it is worth it. If necessary, I will even buy an item or two at retail and resell them at no profit to keep my Search Engine Rankings high.

In other words, if having a particular item in my eBay store is drawing in traffic from outside of eBay, or keeping a customer in my store, I'll pay a little more to carry the item.

Trade Shows

Suppliers, wholesalers, and manufacturers often exhibit their wares at trade shows throughout the country. They can be great opportunities to evaluate products from many different sources, all in one location. It is an excellent way to find new products that have not hit the mass market yet, as some suppliers use the trade show as a means of "testing the market." Also, you may find many smaller suppliers and manufacturers attending these trade shows, attempting to drum up business. This works to your advantage as well, since you may not otherwise become aware of these smaller providers, and they may well have something to offer that is unique.

There are trade shows of all different sizes and scopes. Local, regional, and national trade shows occur on a regular basis, as well as trade shows in other countries. Some of the local trade shows may be open to the public, and you may be able to make some good connections there. Regional shows are often held in major cities. The cost of traveling should be figured into your expected sales, but it may well be worth the time and expense if you have done your research as we recommended.

Trade shows are a good place to get ideas about what is selling in the new product market. Some seasonal national trade shows are Atlanta Market, Dallas Market, Kansas City Market, Javits (New York City) and numerous others. You can find them by going to **www.10times.com** and keying in the country and city where you can attend a trade show. There is a screening process for entry into many trade shows, but many manufacturers do allow home businesses into the shows.

I visit the websites of trade associations or trade shows. For instance, for Garden and Gift category, a search for "Gift Show" might bring you to the Seattle Gift Show. When you visit that site, you find information about the date of the next show, how to register, where it will be, and what vendors will attend the show. If you click the "vendors" tab, you will find a list of the manufacturers and representatives who attend the Gift Show along with their products and contact information. You can do the same thing in your area with a number of keywords. This is a great way to get your foot in the door.

You will probably need to have a tax ID number and be a legitimate business to get in; they are closed to the public. (The tax ID number is usually available from your state revenue department.) Having one works to your advantage. If trade shows were open to the public, you would lose a little bit of your edge. With a tax ID in hand and some inexpensive business cards, you will be able to make a good impression to vendors at trade shows as well as wholesale markets that may exist in your area.

Understand that once you have a tax ID number from your state, you will be required to file periodic sales reports and submit collected sales tax accordingly. Even if you have no sales within your state to report, you must still periodically file the report or face a penalty. At the present time, states do not require sales tax to be collected on sales, which occur out of state. This means that if you live in Florida and

make a sale by eBay to a person living in Colorado, you are NOT required to collect Florida sales taxes and report or submit sales tax to Florida for the sale. In recent years, there has been a movement afoot to require local vendors who sell on the Internet to collect and report sales tax, but this has been repeatedly defeated, due to the difficulty in collecting and reporting the taxes. Which state gets how much of the sale? What is the sales tax rate when multiple jurisdictions are involved? What if the buyer is tax exempt in his or her home state? How does a state police vendors within its borders who are selling interstate via the Internet? But remember, for sales within your home state, you are required to collect and report the sales taxes. Your home state Sales Tax Revenue agency can supply needed information to you in this regard. It all sounds complicated but it's easier to do it than describe it.

Going International

A trip overseas is not as expensive as you think it might be, once you start to spend some time shopping around online. If your travel dates are flexible, you can actually travel overseas quite reasonably. You are very likely to find your best deals when you visit foreign countries, and you will get a great vacation out of it, too.

Many of the wholesalers you deal with get their products from overseas locations, and if you can make those overseas connections yourself, you are bound to get the absolute best prices possible.

Continental Asia I have found is a fine place to find products to resell. Of course, there are factories throughout China that churn out low-quality, mass-produced plastic goods, but there are also very high-quality producers as well, in addition to craftspeople who make some of the most spectacular hand-made items that you will never find near you. Even if you do find them locally, the prices will be far too high.

One such example is the Chatujak Market in Bangkok. This well-known venue is packed full of tourists, locals, and resellers every weekend. It is open to absolutely everyone, and you will have a hard time making your way down the crowded and narrow aisles, but it will be a trip to remember. There is absolutely everything imaginable on offer there. If you go with one particular thing in mind, you will probably find it   but you will also find a dozen other things you never thought of before, as well.

Many of the merchants there are small craftspeople who make the goods themselves, and everything is unique and very inexpensive. The merchants are used to selling to shop owners and retailers who come from all over the world to make large buys, so they will know what you are up to and give you a good deal. There are even shipping companies right there in the market who will help you get your goods back home at a reasonable price.

It is an experience you will never forget, but you have to be a bit of a "power shopper" to survive a day at Chatujak. It is huge, and there are literally thousands of merchant stalls there. No matter how many times you go there, every time you will be surprised at what you see. You can easily get lost several times, but if you do, just go with the flow and enjoy it. There is something new around every corner, and there are plenty of food stalls and small restaurants where you can sit and relax for a while.

Many of the merchants do speak at least some English, but if you can speak a little of their language (or have someone with you who can), chances are you will get a better deal. Even if you do not, it is still possible to negotiate, and it is quite common to strike a bargain just by pointing, gesturing, entering numbers onto a pocket calculator and passing it back and forth.

I made a good profit buying hand-made costume jewelry earrings there (and also in Bangkok's Chinatown district) for ten baht per pair (about $0.25) and reselling them in the States for $5 a pair. I found that buying jewelry, both costume jewelry and finer jewelry from continental Asia was a fine way to make money back home. It is small, and so shipping is not a major problem   and the markup is tremendous. It is common to buy a piece of jewelry in Asia, and then resell it in America for 10 to 20 times your cost.

Be cautious about counterfeit designer goods, however, especially in Asian countries. China and Thailand are notorious for counterfeit and bootleg products. A bazaar in Cambodia I visited had several "Prada" handbags for $5 each; they were no doubt as phony as a $3 bill, despite being quite attractive.

> Buying directly from China? I know I could purchase in bulk directly from overseas, but by the time I acquire the needed license, paperwork, and pay extra in carting services, I can pay a few extra cents to U.S. suppliers, avoid the headache, and have my items sooner.

Direct Manufacturers

In your "wider net" approach, you may also want to consider dealing directly with manufacturers. If the manufacturer wants only high-volume orders and if you are requesting something specialized, you will have to take an indirect approach by going through an intermediary.

Typically, manufacturers work only through large wholesalers, but if you find a manufacturer who makes something you want, you can contact the company directly for a reference to the wholesaler nearest your location so that you can purchase a manageable amount of the product. Some smaller manufacturing operations may be willing to work with you, especially if you are in the same town.

Another type of manufacturer is a custom manufacturer, one that makes specialized goods in limited runs. Of course, the larger the run the better the price you will get, but in many cases, custom mass-production of certain goods is a possibility. An example is the novelty manufacturer. They may, for example, make custom things like mouse pads, shot glasses, or sports items such as caps from a common template but with different images on it.

When dealing with manufacturers and distributors, if you approach them courteously and assure them you will be a repeat buyer and buy in small or large bulk, they are usually more than happy to discount the items that you want to buy and resell.

Most established distributors and manufactures screen their customers and sometimes will not sell to eBay businesses or home-based businesses.

Screening requires documentation of business operation: business account, sales tax/resale number, sometimes even a photograph of the front of the retail shop or building used for business.

Some may set up open accounts based on credit checks. Some will require minimum purchases of quantity or dollar amount. The good news is that some will send merchandise Cash on

> Delivery (COD) or prepaid. As you become a trusted repeat buyer, these costly restrictions may be relaxed.
>
> As you become experienced eBay seller, you may wish to approach manufacturers about selling their outdated or "second" merchandise. You can negotiate for pennies on the dollar, but you will be required to purchase in large lots. Again research on eBay and product knowledge is essential for profit.

One caution about dealing with manufacturers: they, like you, are in business and must make decisions that bear on their longevity. Therefore, you want to research companies that produce something you believe you can sell long-term. Research their history, the resource stability, profits, technology updates, layoffs, relocations, and ability to stay current with competition. Understand their merchandise warranty's too. An eBay seller who says his product has a one year factory warranty will certainly sell more of an identical item similarly priced which does not have a warranty. You and your buyers should feel comfortable with their staying power.

Remanufacturers

EBay is full of remanufactured goods, and they have proven to be a worthwhile and profitable endeavor for many eBay merchants. Remanufacturing means that a manufacturer takes products that have been returned for one reason or another, repairs them or replaces parts, reassembles them, and then repackages them in new packaging. Consumers like them because while they are not exactly new, they are not exactly used either and they cost less than "new" items.

The advantage of a remanufactured item is that it comes directly from the factory, in factory packaging that has not been broken. Remanufactured goods can also be sold at a deep discount over brand new items. As an eBay merchant, you will also have an advantage with remanufactured goods, since most major retailers do not want to handle them, instead opting only for brand new merchandise.

Internet Wholesalers

Of course, as you would with any Internet merchant, do a little checking ahead of time, and do not buy from an Internet vendor who does not give you a physical address and a contact phone number where you can talk to a live person.

Proceed with caution - as you would in dealing with any supplier. But the Internet is after all just a tool, and it is the same tool that forms the very foundation of your eBay business. There are many trustworthy wholesale suppliers that deal on the Internet, so do not overlook this valuable resource.

> The majority of my suppliers are online wholesalers in the United States. I am very happy with the suppliers that I use and have used them for several years. I have never had a problem with items being out of stock and quality is excellent.
>
> You can order from the comfort of your own home and normally have the products on your doorstep within a few days.

EBay wholesalers make up 40 percent of my suppliers. I have found that other eBay sellers also buy from the same wholesaler that I do, but they come in handy at times when the wholesaler may be out of what I need. I can then turn to another eBay seller.

I find that eBay wholesalers are very reliable and dependable. If you form a relationship with these sellers and become repeat buyers, they will discount even more for having you as a loyal return customer. I have been dealing with the same suppliers on eBay for at least four and half years.

Online wholesalers, if they are legitimate, can offer you a tremendous value and a wide selection of products. The Internet wholesaler, **www.Liquidation.com**, for example, as of today's writing, has several attractive items in its massive inventory that would make excellent eBay items. As a company that sources commercial surplus inventory and government surplus assets in an online environment, there are too many options to list: high quality Bluray players for as low as $30, 1000 LCD iPhone protector cases by the lot for $100 per unit, and 100 designer ties for less than $3 each. Even after you factor in the shipping cost, auction-style deals like this just make sense.

EBay Itself as a Source

Better descriptions, better image, regular customers, and outstanding customer service can turn a $10 item purchased on eBay into a $100 item sold on eBay.

By now, you have figured out that eBay is huge, and there are all sorts of sellers on it. Some are professional, some make scads of money, and some just do not know what they are doing. Some are just part-timers, hobbyists, or people who just have a handful of items to sell. It is that latter category of eBay seller that can provide you with hidden treasures.

It is no secret that not everything that is listed on eBay sells. Some things sell for substantially below what they are worth or could have sold if the auction were presented better. Let's say there is an item worth $50. Someone who is unskilled may take a poor picture and may not describe it well. The item gets only two or three bids, and ends up sell-ing for $5. On the other hand, someone could take that same product, take good quality photos of it, and get the full $50 for it.

This presents an opportunity for a little arbitrage. It is cer-tainly possible to buy things on eBay, and then turn right around and resell them on eBay for a profit.

You can make a good living picking up eBay bargains like this and reselling them, once you become adept at picking them out. It takes a little work, since the people with the poor quality listings are not going to be the high-profile power sellers. You may also find tremendous bargains that have been miscategorized. It happens more often than you would think: a seller places an item in the wrong category and gets no bids at all. When you find these miscategorized items, you can put in a low bid and usually win.

There is huge disparity between professional and amateur eBay listings. All sorts of eBay sellers are out there: some are professionals or semi-professionals who make a good living or at least a good secondary living from it, and others who just use eBay as a sort of electronic yard sale to get rid of a few items and make a few extra dollars. The latter category of seller does not have the same high expectations and needs as the professional, and so they will often sell items for lower prices than would someone who is spending eight hours a day at it.

Therefore, it is possible to set up a sort of eBay arbitrage business, a perfect example of pure capitalism at work. You buy low and sell high, using the same marketplace. It is like the stock market. While a stock market investor may buy a stock from the stock exchange for $10 and sell it for $11, an eBay arbitrageur may buy an item on eBay for $10 and sell it for $20, $30, or even $50.

Instead of combing local yard sales every week, these sellers find their goods to buy in the very same venue they are using to sell, and you can make a fine living doing just this.

One good method for determining the best wording is to examine the listings that have fetched the best price for that type of item, copy the text from those auctions, edit it a bit, and call it your own.

Purchasing from established eBay professional dealers can also be lucrative if you buy carefully (buy low, sell high). Recently, I saw a collection of U.S. Mint Commemorative stamps listed for auction. The catalog value of the stamps was about $1,000. Knowing that stamps rarely resell for full catalog value, I placed a bid and won the lot for $75. The album they came in alone was worth the $75 bid. I could have turned around and resold them for between $300-500; but I kept them for myself. The seller was a professional stamp dealer. Ultimately, we were both reasonably happy (me more than the seller, I think). The key here is you must know your product and what it's worth before you bid. Set a maximum you are willing to bid and DO NOT EXCEED it. Sellers on eBay love bidding wars between two or more buyers; it usually leads to the seller making a nice profit and one buyer paying more than he should have. Do not let yourself get caught up in the heat of the auction, this applies to both live auctions that you attend as well as online auctions.

When it comes to online auctions, it is a truism that sooner or later, everything comes up again for sale; if you lose out the first time there will always be another sale down the road, just be patient. Remember that the whole world is participating as buyers or sellers; what may be rare and expensive in the town where you live may be commonplace and cheap 1,000 miles away in another town. Online auctions and sales are the great equalizers. Local supply and demand becomes superfluous when you are dealing in a truly global marketplace.

One Example of Arbitrage

I used to have a generic listing on eBay for an HP 15 Pavilion Laptop with 1.0 GHz processor, 4GB RAM, and 500 GB hard drive, CD-ROM and Windows Vista. I would list several of these, having built up an inventory of them, and if necessary, would exceed (but never fall short of) the stated specs. For example, I may provide an HP 13 with 4GB RAM, otherwise the same, if necessary, or maybe a 2.0 GHz processor in place of the 1.0. Sometimes more — *never less*.

For each laptop sold, I would buy a corresponding unit so I would keep up my inventory level. On more than one occasion, I would receive a laptop in the morning, open it up, check it out, perhaps tweak it a bit, maybe install a modem, remove a program, or some other small task, and ship it out the same afternoon in the very same box. This technique involves work, some considerable capital involvement, and some risk, but, in this instance, it normally returns $1,000 a week. The idea is to turn around 10 units a week while making a profit of around $100 on each. And you can do this all on eBay. You can certainly find inexpensive laptops in many different places, but it is quite possible to develop a thriving laptop business buying and selling them on eBay alone.

The key is to scoop up the units listed by the amateurs, while copying the text and style from the pros. Buy low, sell high, and turn them around quickly. It is almost easier done than said. Who said making money is hard to do? If you are willing to put in the time and experiment with creative strategies, you can make excellent returns.

When dealing with second-hand PCs and laptops, buyers are usually interested in a bargain, and while they probably have something in mind, often are not particular as to the details. So long as they get the brand they asked for and it has at least the same amount of power and features you advertised, you will have satisfied customers. It was astonishingly rare for anyone to inquire as to the model number of a particular unit. Whenever this happened, I would simply isolate a unit from my small, ever-revolving inventory, cite that model, and hold it for the bidder who made the inquiry. Otherwise, it was just reel 'em in and roll 'em out.

I would usually have two or even three different "models" with specific sets of specs. The trick with laptops as always is where to get the hard drives, and more specifically, where to get the hard drive *caddy*. In the corporate and government worlds, when laptops are traded in, the hard drives in their caddies are typically removed in a most unceremonious manner, and literally whacked with a hammer, so that no sensitive data falls into the wrong hands.

Therefore, since these caddies are proprietary, they can be quite difficult to get and often command high prices. If the laptop model is ubiquitous, one can buy aftermarket caddies (I used to get them at around $18 each delivered, in lots of 5). It's kind of salty, but resurrecting a laptop from parts and pieces can be lucrative indeed.

Strike When Lightning Hits

There are some rare and very lucky occasions where an individual or company has a large volume of salable goods, and for whatever procedural or accounting reasons does not want them and is not interested in selling them. Every day, companies, stores, and manufacturers throw out perfectly good quality items, and if you are able to tap into them, they can be sold on eBay.

My very first eBay experience came when I was driving a coffee truck temporarily. The company had just won the account of a major grocery chain in the Mid-Atlantic region. We were required to purchase every single bean from the outgoing company at their cost, $5.77 per pound. When the outgoing company realized this, they stuffed the bins full, even going so far as to hide sealed

five-pound foil bags behind displays to extract the maximum payment for the road. When we took over the stores, we weighed the beans in the presence of the store manager, who then issued a credit memo.

Incredibly, we were throwing the beans into the dumpster! As a marketing major and hard-core java junkie, I was appalled. I quickly decided to rescue those precious beans from their disgraceful fate, diverting them to my empty truck.

On the second day, realizing that when I wrote a credit memo to the store manager, it had the same legal status as a check, making the beans the property of our company, which had no interest in them at all, effectively making the beans mine. And since I was going back home with an empty 14-foot van, loading it up with unwanted coffee beans started to make sense.

The company hired more temporary help to demolish the outgoing company's displays and to dump the beans. I implored them please keep the beans separate - do not mix the flavors. And label the bags with a magic marker. MJ for mocha java, CR for chocolate raspberry, and mark the decaf.

I ended up with, who knows exactly, but best estimate would be around 1,400 pounds of premium oily fresh gourmet beans, much of which was hermetically sealed in five-pound bags, for a total cost of - nothing! I gave away shopping bags of the stuff to neighbors, family, friends, and still had well over half a ton.

I also acquired the official gold and red foil bags, which were still shrink-wrapped in bundles of 100. The boxes in which I delivered the incoming bean for our company held eight five-pound bags, and I dropped the empty boxes off at my house on the way back to the barn - it was not off my route. I removed the logos from the boxes and listed the coffee on eBay at $2 per pound, with shipping of $8. Shipping cost me $4 to $5 going east and $10 to $12 to the West Coast, so the cost averaged out as a wash. The boxes were free, so the $8 per case shipping was truly rock bottom.

I ended up getting around $2.50 to 3.50 per pound, all profit of course. Many people emailed me inquiring whether I had this flavor or that flavor, and several folks bought 50 or 60 pounds each.

The coffee truck job only lasted long enough to stock the stores, so when the coffee I had sold on eBay was gone, I realized that I did not have a job. But that is the nature of eBay, and indeed, the nature of almost any venture.

Retail is transitory; you take advantage of what you have, when you have it, and then move onto the next thing. However, I had learned how to use eBay, so I was just browsing and stumbled on a seller in Philadelphia who had an old Compaq I 60 MHz desktop (It had 8MB RAM, and a 0.5GB hard drive, but it did have the latest version of Windows — no CD-ROM though). Overall, I paid $19 for my first PC, bought a monitor also on eBay, and sold it through an ad in the local paper for $160! I know that a lot of those specs are now outdated, but I've been in the eBay business for a long time since then and the principles are still the same. If you pay attention to all your options, buy smart, and sell smart, you can always make over 700 percent net profit just like I did for my first PC sell. The numbers have changed, but people and the game are still the same.

I was buying PCs and monitors on eBay, selling through ads in local papers, and had won an auction on a 17-inch monitor, when I noticed that the seller was only eight miles from me. I called and asked if I could pick it up to save on shipping, and he said, "Sure." I walked into the place and stopped dead in my tracks.

There were stacks of Dell and Compaq PCs taller than I am. There were dozens and dozens of stacks. That was the day I met Stevie, and he would be my sole supplier of PCs and PC parts to sell on eBay for years to come. His main sources are governments, schools, and corporations that buy new computers regularly and need the old ones hauled away.

Chapter 4

Becoming a Consignment Shop

a more recent innovation among eBay enthusiasts is to create a consignment shop. Using this business model, you do not actually sell any products of your own, and you do not have to find them. Other people bring you their own items; you sell them on their behalf, and take a commission.

The advantage to doing this is that you save all that time you would otherwise spend trying to seek out all those wonderful items. You just have to open your doors and wait for people to bring them to you. Of course, you do not get to take all the profit, but this has turned out to be quite a lucrative venture for some eBay folks.

EBay used to formalize this arrangement by calling you a "Trading Assistant." This practice was halted some time ago; apparently there may have been legal ramifications that eBay did not want to incur by formally qualifying some sellers as Trading Assistants. While there are no more Trading Assistants, that doesn't mean you cannot create and operate your own consignment operation.

No Inventory

In an eBay consignment operation, the inventory you carry is not your own. You are only holding other peoples' products.

In a normal eBay business, storage is always a problem, and some people, after several months in the business, find their closets, storage rooms, basements, and even living rooms and bedrooms quickly  becoming overrun with products. That is called "early eBay house." It can become a serious problem if you do not have a separate, dedicated space for storage. Also, there will naturally be some products you have that will not sell.

What do you do with those products? Let them sit around in a spare room until it is someone's birthday, or Christmas comes around and you can give them away? In the meantime, they take up space, and there are only so many items you can give away. In an eBay consignment operation, when a product does not sell, you return it to its owner. It no longer has to take up space in your home or shop.

The Consignment Business Model

In this type of business, you gain the advantage of not having to pay for your inventory. You are simply making a deal with other people to sell their goods on their behalf, and then you take a fee and commission for your trouble. When they bring you their goods, you do not have to pay for them since you are not really buying them. It is a great way to get started in eBay without having to put out any significant investment in product stock.

Many of these types of operations have a standard brick-and-mortar storefront, which requires some up-front capital. However, you do not have to start out that way. You can do consignments easily from your home. The advantage to having a storefront, of course, is that people will see you more easily and become aware of your presence in the neighborhood.

You will get a certain amount of walk-in traffic just because people have driven by and seen your sign. On the other hand, you can just as easily start out in your home and avoid the up-front expense of a storefront shop. Create some fliers and signs, advertise in the local paper, and use word-of-mouth.

Simple word-of-mouth may not work in all businesses, but it works quite well for eBay consignment operations. Everyone has something to get rid of and make a little money at the same time, but few actually get around to listing it on eBay. Once you start telling your circle of friends, relatives, and acquaintances that you will sell things for them, word will get around very quickly, and you will have plenty of items to launch your business.

Consignment sales for companies are another twist on avoiding storage, and it is a good way to find a wide range of products to sell on eBay. Consignment selling here means that you offer to sell an item that belongs to a company for a percentage of the sales price. You can charge up to half the selling price plus fees for smaller items - like household goods and clothing - and about 15 percent for larger items like cars, boats, and backhoes.

Most businesses are cluttered with used equipment, returned items, or liquidated products that they would like to get rid of, but have no time to do so or no experience online. Contact all the businesses in your area and offer to list their excess goods on eBay for a piece of the action. You will be a blessing if you can help them get rid of this merchandise. The money you make is not bad either since they pay the eBay fees.

One risk people face when selling on eBay is that they may end up spending more on eBay listing fees than they make in profits. This can easily happen if you list several items but sell only a few. If you use a consignment model, your customer, who is the owner of the product you are selling, pays the eBay fees.

Your contract with your customer can take many different forms, but a good way to structure it is to say that first, if the item is not sold, it will be returned to the customer, and the customer will pay for all listing fees.

If the item sells, you will subtract the listing fees and shipping fees, plus either a flat fee or a commission from the proceeds.

Pros and Cons of Using a Drop Shipper

Being an Intermediary

Place a big first order. Tell them the truth. Offer exclusivity. Be polite.

Sometimes it pays to be an intermediary. You can be an eBay merchant and not have to get your hands dirty actually handling products with the help of a drop shipping company. It provides products that you sell, and when your orders come in, the drop shipper fulfills the order for you and puts your company's label on the box. You never have to touch, or even see, the product.

Since wholesale buying often requires a great deal of storage space, you may want to look into the use of a reliable drop shipper, if for no other reason than to avoid having to deal with warehousing, product picking, inventory records, and other ordinary time-consuming elements of the fulfillment process. This is a system in which you *sell* the products and the drop shipper *stores and then ships it for you*.

Naturally, there are some inherent limitations with this approach. Countless others may be offering the same thing. Drop shippers make their money by getting small merchants to offer their catalog under their own name.

But if you are one of those people who does not want to package, ship, and keep track of multiple items, then drop shipping is the only way to go. One of the most comprehensive lists of drop shippers that you can access is a Drop Ship Source Directory. You can easily eliminate pointless middlemen by simply using such directories. The list of names you will obtain from a Drop Ship Source Directory is by far the most up-to-date list that you will find, and

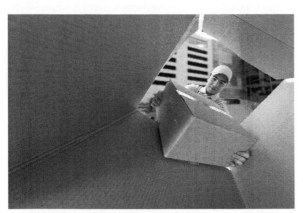

it is very useful for any and all Internet businesses you run.

*Cautionary Note: While drop shipping is a legitimate business and it can be very profitable, there are also many drop ship scams out there. Due to this fact, I will list a few verified options here:

- **Salehoo.com** (For an annual fee of only $67, they boast a directory of over 8,000 genuine, verified wholesale suppliers)

- **Worldwidebrands.com** (lifetime fee of $299, ONLY publisher of wholesale product sourcing information certified by Ebay)

- **Thomasnet.com** (provides listings for thousands of suppliers, somewhat difficult to navigate and does not guarantee willingness of suppliers to offer drop-shipping arrangement but it is free)

A purported drop shipper may merely be an intermediary who claims he is the actual supplier. Also, the goods you are representing may be substandard. You lose an element of quality control when using a drop shipper since you are not personally inspecting the items. It is very easy to make a poor quality product look good in a picture. However, when customers get the product, and it is not what they expected, they will not blame the invisible drop shipper. They will blame you. Avoid drop ship frauds and establish an online business or eBay presence by using only reputable, reliable drop shippers.

A variation of this process is a fulfillment service, which does not supply the products, but takes your products, which you have personally selected, stores them, and completes the fulfillment process on your behalf. Numerous reputable suppliers are more than willing to do drop shipping or fulfillment on your behalf.

They may require an account set-up fee that you will need to pay, so you will need to be prepared for some initial investment, but always carefully investigate all related costs before agreeing to anything in writing.

A simple online search is a very good way to find suppliers who do drop shipping, but understand many companies who are far more interested in taking money *from you* as opposed to helping you make money for yourself. This is a very shortsighted approach on their part because when you make money, they do too. However, as in all occupations, many do not understand this simple principle. Find a drop shipper who is reputable, willing to talk to you in person (and not just through email), and who will send you actual physical samples of products for your review before you buy in bulk.

Some issues to be certain to clarify before starting a business relationship with any drop shipper are these:

- How much will they charge you for the merchandise, including any handling charges they might pass on to you for storing, packaging, and shipping the item?

- Precisely how will the charges be processed? Are you required to pay as you go, as they ship each item, or will they send you an invoice monthly?

- Do they accept returns directly from your buyers in the event that the merchandise should be damaged?

When you use a drop shipper, you transfer the inherent risks of buying merchandise, shipping it, and storing it to a third party. You then become a stockless retailer who has no inventory to carry. Done with care, this is an economical, cost-effective way for you to do business.

The following steps outline an efficient method to working with most drop shippers via eBay, and has become the standard for doing so:

1. Agree to sell a drop shipper's products on eBay or on your own web store. Be sure you have checked out their terms before you agree to anything in writing to be certain there is no minimum purchase at the time of signing.

2. Select the products that you wish to sell from their inventory. For this example, suppose the item you selected costs $7.97. The supplier gives you descriptive copy and images to make your marketing easier.

3. Post the item online and then wait for someone to purchase it. You will be selling this item for $19.99 plus shipping.

4. When your buyer had paid for the item, email the drop shipper and pay for it with your credit card.

5. The drop shipper packages and then ships the item to the customer for you with your own label on the package.

6. When all goes well, the purchase arrives quickly and as described. You make a handsome profit and get positive feedback.

The drop shipper's website will provide you with ready-made descriptions and digital images of each product. Check ahead of time to make sure you have permission to re-use this copy from their catalog, but most do allow for this. However, you and everyone else who sells that particular item on eBay will have the same digital photos and the very same descriptive copy.

By all means, do yourself a favor and take your own pictures and write your own description. If you are selling an item and there are 1,000 other listings for the same item, each with identical text and pictures, you are not going to have much luck in making a sale, and when you do, you will not get a good price for it. At least take the same copy and rewrite it, alter the font, colors, and otherwise maintaining the same winning character, but with a new and different look and feel. That way, you have a fighting chance to rise above the "sea of sameness" on eBay.

Drop shipping works very well for Web-based retail entities. Web stores can be linked directly to the drop shipper's computer system to transfer shipping and payment data. However, when you are selling with the big boys on eBay, it is quite another thing. Although the drop shipper may have thousands of items in their catalog, and they encourage you to try to sell as many of them as  possible, it is just not practical to lift hundreds of products out of a drop shipper's catalog and post them on eBay. The fees will sabotage you, your sales ratio will be terribly low, and your profit margins will be slim.

Listing many items on eBay can cost a ton of money and may run your expenses through the roof before you even make a penny of profit. You cannot just pick an item from a drop shipper and shotgun hundreds of auctions without losing money; that is, unless the product is selling at a very healthy profit. Even if that were the case, you could be certain of encountering another eBay seller buying directly from the same manufacturer and undercutting your price.

Instead, review multiple drop shippers' catalogs and carefully select items that you think have a high resale value and fit together into a particular category or niche.

Some drop shippers require you to sign in and even pay a fee before you can see their catalog. Avoid them. It is one thing to dip a toe in the water and sign up for a free newsletter - or even register with a particular drop shipper's site - but it is something else altogether to be required to pay just to see what the drop shipper intends to offer. You should never pay anything in advance just to sign up with a drop shipping service. You should be able to give the drop shipping service a trial run before you commit to spending much money. That said, after you see the catalog, it may well be worthwhile to order a few single items to evaluate the quality before you list them.

Thousands of Web companies and drop shippers are just itching to help you establish your online business. Ever since the Internet became a commercial tool, the idea of Internet wealth has become very attractive. It is true that many sellers have reaped wealth on legitimate Internet pursuits. You naturally want your piece of that action, and there are companies, drop shippers, publishers, and promoters of various schemes who will tell you how to do it for a fee. Most of them are excellent companies with legitimate backgrounds; however, there are others who sincerely hope you do not have a clue about what you are doing. They are betting heavily that you will be just desperate enough to send them a nominal payment to help you get your fair share of the "millions to be made online."

Consider these points when choosing drop shippers to work with:

- A little skepticism is healthy. The wise person would think twice when encountering a website that boasts that they can drop ship thousands of different products. Only mega stores carry thousands of items. Most drop shipping services do not. A smaller product line may indicate that the drop shipper indeed does have the merchandise ready to ship and is not relying on ordering it from another wholesaler on your behalf. The drop shipper with "thousands of items" may be nothing more than a little shop that orders products from other wholesalers, a business model that may work very well for them, but it causes your customer delays in getting an order. Shipping delays on eBay sales can be the kiss of death for you as a seller. EBay requires you to specify shipping times on your listing. If you fail to comply with that

shipping time repeatedly, eBay can suspend or bar you from future selling.

- Beware of long lines of distribution. Drop shippers are often merely intermediaries who act as a broker for several different underlying sources. For example, some drop shippers may obtain their products from yet another list of middlemen who buy from a line of brokers upon brokers until actually contacting someone who directly buys from manufacturers. The actual line of distribution can get still even longer, which means that many different people are making a profit from the sale of your item long before you even purchase it "at wholesale." If even only one other intermediary acquires the item directly from the distributor or even from the manufacturer, that competitor may easily beat your selling price and make for himself the profit that should have been yours. It is a good policy to verify with the drop shipper that they do indeed stock the merchandise they sell on their premises.

- Do not believe their claims of uniqueness and high value automatically. Drop shippers will often claim in their catalogs that a particular item has a very high resale value, when in fact, it does not. If you see an item you would consider reselling, do some research before ordering. Look for the item on the Web and see if there are other places selling it. Keep an eye out in your shopping when you go to your local department stores. Do not be surprised if that item the catalog lists as having a "retail value of $49.99" is being sold by other eBay vendors for $10. You may even see the very same product at a department store discount bin, or worse yet, at your local dollar store.

Many reliable wholesalers will drop ship for you. When you find a drop shipper who also functions as a wholesaler (or vice versa), try to find one who is professional and especially one that has a good track record (You can verify a wholesaler's track record by asking the business for references relating to their past experience with drop shipping or contacting current customers directly to get a clear, updated opinion). Look for reliable, experienced buyers who get premium merchandise and who can handle pro-level business issues such as resale permits and sales tax numbers.

What happens if you sell your item, go to the distributor's site, and find it is not in stock? Before you panic, by all means, call the drop shipper. It is possible that they still have the items in the warehouse and they simply took it off the website because it was running low.

If that is not the case, you will have to contact your buyers and admit that the items they bought are currently not on hand with your supplier. It is imperative that you email or call your customers directly in this situation; they very well may not be as angry as they might be if you had just emailed this information, so call them if the phone number is available on their eBay account and email as well for a backup. It would be wise to offer to refund their money in full immediately - possibly even send some kind of consolation offering such as adding the option of free shipping or a certain friendly but manageable percent discount on their next order. Someone else's foul-up may net you negative feedback. That risk is inherent in employing drop shipping as a routine business practice.

- When you use drop shipper, be aware that they become the intermediary who will be getting the majority of your profit.

- To make a profit using a drop shipper, you may have to raise your prices above the eBay market place for that product, and buyers will go on to the next seller who offers it for less.

- Will the drop shipper have that product that you are selling for them on eBay in stock? Will they ship as fast as you? You are putting your good reputation in the hands of others.

- You have to pay a drop shipper for using their products and services and may incur either a monthly or annual fee.

- Like any other successful business, eBay is no different. It requires hard work, and dedication. It will pay off! The old saying is, "If you want it done the right way, do it yourself."

- Never pay a supplier, such as drop-shipper, a fee or membership fee to buy their product.

- You do not have to buy in bulk. There are plenty of suppliers that allow you to make only a minimum purchase.

- Start out buying small bulk to make sure you are happy with the quality and customer service of that supplier.

- Be sure to check the return policy of any supplier in case you do get an item that does not meet your standards or an item becomes unavailable prior to shipping.

- Check to see if they are located in the United States.

- Send the supplier an email to see what their response time is or even make a call to them and ask questions.

The most disheartening experiences in connecting with suppliers are to purchase quantity items or opt into any drop-shipping contracts before they have been thoroughly researched for marketability on eBay. This can lead to disaster on eBay and that is not fun for any potential eBay entrepreneur.

There are several things to remember about finding suppliers or manufacturers to buy product from for eBay sales.

1. There are many variables in selling on eBay so before you purchase anything remember to research similar items by checking eBay existing and completed auctions for price comparisons. Completed Listings can be found on the left toolbar on any eBay Listing page.

2. Remember it is the "bottom line" that counts - how much profit you make from any item you sell. Always keep that in mind before negotiating any price or purchasing any quantity of product.

3. Check out your supply source carefully if you are looking for a long-term relationship with a supplier or

manufacturer. Be careful of any supply relationship where you are not in control of the merchandise. It is your reputation on the line if a supplier/drop shipper is out of an item you have contracted to sell on eBay. You will need to know the particulars of any merchandise you are selling - quality, weight, design, color - so you want to have it "in hand" for best results.

4. Scams proliferate in drop shipping and off shore shipping offers so the bottom line is, "if it sounds too good to be true, it probably is." If you have any questions about the legitimacy of a company, you can check with your state attorney general's fraud division by keying in your state and Attorney General (example, Kansas Attorney General) in a search engine and then click on their fraud division. Get the number from the site and call the office. If you wish to purchase offshore, it is best to discuss it with your Small Business Development Center: **http://www.sba. gov/tools/local-assistance/sbdc** (click on your state for one near you). Purchasing offshore requires expertise and is not for inexperienced eBay Sellers.

Being a Drop Shipper

If you want to be a drop shipper for a company, they will provide you with a complete, payment-enabled website and the merchandise to sell on the site.

You can sell the merchandise on eBay auctions. You select the design of the site, the products you want to sell, and they do the rest. They can show you how to set up an online payment system, help you register a domain name, offer technical support, and more

It is up to you to market the site and drive customers to it, but in some cases the companies will even help you do that with free search engine optimization and marketing tips. This is the fastest way to get your drop ship business up and running in just days.

Chapter 6

B2B, Liquidations, and Dedicated Manufacturers

B2B Exchange

The idea of an electronic exchange is not unique to eBay. There are many different types of exchanges, and some of them can be very useful in managing your eBay business and acquiring goods to sell. There are some electronic exchanges that specialize in matching up businesses with other businesses — for example, matching retailers with wholesalers. These are called B2B (business-to-business) exchanges, and they can give your eBay business a big boost.

You may be able to tap into some of these exchanges to get unheard of rates on products that you can resell on eBay or find new and interesting products to sell that you have never heard of before.

Participation in B2B exchanges has become one of the fastest growing ways for businesses to augment their client base beyond their local or regional markets. A good B2B exchange will offer direct contact with thousands of potential buyers in a single location. For many new participants in a B2B exchange, it seems like a goldmine. They discover an unexpected trove of ready-made clients without much effort on their part. Of course, there are countless other wonderful benefits that companies can realize from participating in a B2B exchange.

As an eBay merchant, the B2B exchange will not be the place to find customers, but it will be a great place for you to find things to sell to your own customers on eBay.

Liquidations

Liquidation sales are a great way to find inventory. Your local stores may have liquidation sales, closeout sales, or liquidation auctions. Large department stores face a tremendous amount of competition in today's marketplace, and you will often find them going out of business and holding liquidation sales. Toward the end of their sales cycle, discounts are extremely deep, and you can pick up brand new items at low cost, which you can easily resell. Liquidation auctions are also a very reliable source of inventory.

The types of auctions I go to are inventory liquidation or going out of business auctions. I have had mixed success at them. It depends on the other bidders. If there are buyers who will pay anything for the merchandise and bid things sky high, I go home after hours of work empty handed. If, on the other hand, my fellow attendees are looking to resell, as I do, I can buy items to resell for a profit.

My strategy is to spend as much time as possible *before* the auction researching the inventory. I want to know if I can sell it and how much I can sell it for. I find out how many have sold on eBay in the recent past. More than once, I have been up late into the night before the auction researching completed listings.

If possible, I will preview the items and take notes. The day of the auction, I know what lot numbers I want to bid on and have my maximum bid written down. When the auctioneer is trying to cajole us into higher bids, I have my top price in front of me. Having it on paper keeps me from being drawn into a bidding war.

Even stores that sell liquidated items can be a good source. If there is one nearby, check out the inventory, make notes on any likely item (price, ISBN number, color, size), and look for it on recently sold items on eBay. If you strike gold researching one thing that is in plentiful supply in your local store, figure the mailing cost, list it for three days (preferably ending on Sunday evening), and if it sells, go back, buy it if you did not buy it at first sighting, and send it to its new owner. If it proves successful, buy and sell more, in that order.

Dedicated Manufacturers

You have seen that one of the best ways to become successful on eBay is to find something that no one else has. Unique craft items and rare specialty products are a natural for eBay. But where do you find these sorts of things? It is not necessary to contract with a high-end manufacturer and pay hundreds of thousands of dollars.

Hit the flea markets, looking for crafters who make highly shippable, light, original items. Buy one unit as a sample, photograph it, list it, and buy more as needed.

Ask them about eBay - they may not be into it - not everyone is. They may not know how to list an item, or they may be familiar with eBay and decide to devote their time to the production end.

In a flea market setting, the opportunity is there to acquire an entire army of crafters to supply you with a diverse line of products from picture frames to macramé, from leather belts to fishing lures, all original, all handmade, and not available anywhere else at any price. There are, for example, plenty of people who make their own jewelry, some of it quite attractive and highly profitable. This approach allows you to buy on an as-needed basis while setting yourself up for volume discounts later as sales increase. You can find these people at local craft shows, flea markets, and festivals, and they will be happy for your business.

By arranging a quantity discount, the enterprising online marketer can have a never ending supply of these items flowing into his online supply chain in an orderly fashion, and quite possibly, without putting out any upfront cash.

Chapter 7

Buying Closeout
Merchandise

any people buy overstocked or closeout merchandise for resale. It is a successful technique especially used by small businesses that sell on eBay. You can earn large profits if you buy carefully. You want to buy only desirable merchandise. Sometimes merchandise shows up with closeout dealers because it would not sell in a store. These items should be avoided. Look for merchandise that did not sell for economic reasons, not because the merchandise was poor. Some examples:

- Seasonal goods
- Store closing or bankruptcy
- Obsolete goods replaced by newer products
- Customer returns after the holidays but not warranty or defect returns

One of the best places to find great deals on merchandise is through "closeout" dealers. Another name for these outfits is Liquidators.

Most wholesale merchandise comes brand new from wholesalers. However, closeout merchants may deal both in brand new merchandise such as those pieces gotten from overstocks. Additionally, vendors of closeout merchandise sometimes deal in returns and used goods.

Advantages and Disadvantages

There are two primary advantages to buying closeout merchandise. First, closeout merchandise is inexpensive. It has the advantage that you can generally obtain a product far cheaper than if you went through a non-closeout vendor. Generally, the merchandise tends to be high quality, but the price is cut or marked way down for clearance.

You can usually sell these items on eBay or at flea markets, where the regular eBay or flea-market buyer expects great deals, yet does not need or require the same vendors to sell the same sorts of goods month after month. Therefore, closeout merchandise frequently makes its way to eBay where everyone wins.

There are two basic drawbacks in buying closeout merchandise: limited stock and the possibility of receiving low quality merchandise.

You usually cannot make a stable inventory out of buying closeout merchandise since the product availability fluctuates. That does not have to be a big drawback, however, especially if you are an eBay merchant. You have the advantage of product flexibility. You should use it to your advantage. People expect a department store to carry the same merchandise, day in and day out, but if you are an eBay merchant, you have more flexibility, and it is precisely that flexibility that is going to make you successful. If

you deal in closeout merchandise, you can make a business out of selling a particular *type* of product, but you certainly do not need to stock the exact make and model on a regular basis.

Most important, a buyer of closeout goods needs to be on guard against the possibility of buying merchandise that is irregular, damaged, or somehow has a low resale value. The chances increase with goods that have been returned. For the most part, returned goods obtained from a reputable closeout vendor have no problems. People return them because they wanted a newer model, ordered the wrong thing or the wrong color, or any number of other reasons that have nothing to do with the quality of the product. Obviously though, your closeout supplier should have a policy regarding products that are faulty. If they sell you a pallet load of alarm clocks that do not buzz, phones that do not ring, toasters that do not toast, or printers that do not print, they should be willing to take them back.

You can circumvent these problems by dealing only with reputable closeout dealers. How to find them will be discussed in the next section.

Last, if possible, it may be worth your time to go to the source to inspect the merchandise in person; and thus geographical locale may be an important deciding factor when you are looking to buy closeout merchandise. In lieu of a physical visit if that is not possible, see if you can buy only one of an item before making a large buy, so you can inspect it for quality control.

Remember too that if a product warranty is of importance to you or your buyer, you may not get a warranty with closeout merchandise. If in doubt, contact the original manufacturer to determine if original factory warranties still apply or have they been voided by the manufacturer. As seller, you will ultimately be responsible to your buyer for defects and failures of the product. If there is no warranty, you should so state in your listing so that there is no confusion on the part of your buyer after the sale is completed.

Product from Reputable Dealers: How to Know

You want your first experience buying closeout merchandise to be positive. How do you know what to buy and from whom?

Say you are new to the reselling game. You are not even sure about what sells or whether you can make a profit. Every retailer and especially the larger ones, engages in industrial espionage to some degree. While some people do get into trouble with illegal methods, espionage for the most part is legal and quite ordinary. It is nothing more than information gathering.

Suppose there are two grocery stores, one on each end of town. They sell pretty much the same sorts of items. You will notice that in such a case, although there will be some differences in prices, you will end up spending about the same in either place. That is because each store will send an employee to the other store to compare prices. You too, need to know what your competition is getting for the same product.

One of the best places to obtain price information for what sells on eBay, is on eBay itself. If you have a crate of Canon Bubble Jet printers, log onto eBay, enter the product, and find out their usual selling price. An excellent way to find out pricing information is to research that product on **http://uk.andale.com/corp/products/research.jsp**. Once at the site, put your item in the search box, and you will generate a listing, which tells you what others have gotten for comparable merchandise in the recent past. The Andale research tool is free for the first three searches and then costs £7.95 (approximately $12.75 USD) each month thereafter. It is quite useful and straightforward.

After you have researched what sells, you then want to find out where to buy the merchandise. An excellent resource to the latest closeouts and liquidations from many national suppliers, as well as a means of connecting closeout buyers with closeout suppliers, is **www.closeoutcentral.com**. CloseoutCentral is a free online closeout merchandise locator in which you can either A) join their email list of buyers emailed daily with the latest closeout opportunities or B) have yourself added to their Seller Directory and have your closeout deals posted on their website as well as be included in their daily mail. By utilizing CloseoutCentral forum, you will be able to contact the 100+ sellers in their Seller Directory and thus access their contact info, their address and view all of the lots each company currently has for sale.

Do I get what I expected when ordering goods? If I have done my research - Yes. When working with a sales representative, I can inspect a product before ordering it. If I do not get to see a sample and I am not happy with the product after I get it, most companies will accept returns from a dissatisfied buyer. If you are working with a company that wants to be in business tomorrow, they will not "bait and switch" their resellers.

Chapter 8

Wholesale Misconceptions

There Is Wholesale and Then There Is Wholesale

People often tend to think that working with a real wholesale supplier means that they will immediately be able to sell products for less than their competition for an unlimited amount of time. However, even when using a genuine wholesale supplier, you are going to eventually find some stores selling products at a "retail" price that is lower than your suppliers' "wholesale" price. That's because IT IS ALL ABOUT VOLUME. As an individual eBay seller, you can command only a certain amount of power with wholesalers. Since mega commercial store chains can buy in such enormous volume, it is certainly possible that they will often get a better price than you will. However, this does not make your wholesale efforts any less fruitless, for playing smart and utilizing the personal aspect of your business has as many pros as it does cons. You just need to be aware of both.

There are good reasons for the relationship between higher volumes and lower costs, and it is important to understand them to be able to sell successfully on the Internet or anywhere else.

It happens for a variety of reasons, the most common of which is that the retailer with the "lower than wholesale" price is a large operation that bought thousands of the product at a dirt-cheap quantity price break and qualified for huge wholesaler rebates. There are simply different levels of wholesale. Your wholesale price is not the same as the mega store's wholesale price.

The term "wholesale" is relative, no matter who your distributors are or how you found them. What you are getting as a small business is a wholesale supplier's genuine "first level" wholesale price.

For example, one factory-direct wholesale supplier has an initial wholesale price for 1 to 50 tennis rackets, then a lower price for 51 to 100, and then a lower price for the next higher quantity level. When dealing with single item orders in your home business, you are obviously going to be getting the "first level" – the worst – wholesale price.

Again, wholesale is a relative term. Yes, genuine wholesale suppliers do sell at significant discounts below manufacturer's suggested retail price (MSRP). However, you have to watch what you sell. Electronics, for example, are a very tough market, because everyone is trying to sell electronics on the 'net right now.

All these people are so busy trying to undercut each other that they have driven the market price of these items down so low it's very difficult to make a profit, even at wholesale.

For example, if the MSRP for a sound system is $150 and it is available at "wholesale" for $70, which is a 54 percent discount off MSRP. That is a good profit, right? However, the fact is, the MSRP means nothing, and there are larger retailers, and even smaller retailers, who sell at significantly under the MSRP. With everyone getting roughly the same price break, there are people who are ruining the market for everyone else by selling that product for, say, $75, thinking they will undercut everyone else and make money by selling volume. Soon everyone else sees this and tries the same thing. Eventually, the Internet "market price" for this sound system becomes $75, and everyone is flooding the market with it at that price. That is such a small profit margin that product is no longer worth the effort for anyone.

Even though the product is available initially at a great wholesale price, its market value is ruined by those who wrongly assume that the only way to sell is to have the absolute lowest price anywhere. But the thing about selling at the lowest price is that it only works for a handful of retailers. A mega store can sell 1,000 Blue-ray players a day. If you are selling one a week, it is not worth your time.

Selling is much more of an art than simply having low pricing. If selling something were just a matter of having the lowest prices, Wal-Mart would be the only store on Earth. Selling is a mixture of choosing the right product, or combination of products, to sell on eBay. It is giving the customer some little value-added bonus at your site by providing the best customer service that you can.

All these efforts help customers trust you, so that they are willing to spend a little more to buy from you.

As an eBay entrepreneur, remember to choose comparison areas very carefully. Too many people simply go to the big search engines and look for the absolute lowest price on earth, and then give up on selling that item if they cannot beat it while they need to be comparing customer service: return policies, easy contact, answers to customers' questions, solid packaging, and fast mailing. Alternatively, you can simply sell the models that others are NOT selling. After you begin to earn some profit, you can then start to buy and stock the better sellers in quantity, lowering your price.

The big superstores, both in their brick-and-mortar stores and in their online sites, offer the lowest prices. They sell thousands of the product, and get them at the best wholesale price. This allows them to sell at a lower price. Go around them. Sell models that they do not, from the same brand names. You do not have to go purposely head-to-head with the big superstores. They do not carry every product ever made. Sell something in the same general brand and product lines that they are not offering.

Besides the reasons mentioned above, there are also too many people who buy entire pallet loads of last year's closeouts, liquidations, and refurbished goods, and claim that they are new. They get that junk at "rock bottom" prices, and of course, sell them dirt-cheap, fooling the customer (and other Internet retailers) into thinking that they have the corner on the best wholesale prices around, when they simply do not.

The important thing is to work effectively within the framework of available products and prices and work with those who have millions of dollars available to stock inventory.

That is what they did to earn those millions in the first place. You can do it, too. It is frustrating to be just starting out and thinking that you cannot succeed because of competition from large stores, but that is just not true. People do succeed at it. You just have to be willing to be flexible and to make serious decisions for the good of your business. You may have to give up selling certain products that you personally like to make money on other products you do not.

It is very important to form a legal business. It is the only way to work with genuine wholesale suppliers. Most wholesalers will not work with you at all if you have not made yourself into a legal business and have a tax ID number.

If you purchase a product at some expense, say televisions, for example, and find that you are being undersold, combine it with another product such as extra speakers with their own price break and try again for a profit. As they say in the United States Marine Corps, *"Adapt, improvise and overcome."* When you are in business you will always have to compete. It is all part of sales – on eBay or anywhere else.

Scams and Tricks to Avoid

Unscrupulous companies and suppliers often see the small-business person who wants to work at home as a prime target, and there are thousands of "work at home," "get rich quick," and "learn how to get rich on eBay" scams out there. For the most part, you will only lose your money.

Simply search "work at home jobs" on the Internet and see what comes up. You will be swamped with job offers, but when you try and look at them, most of the sources require you enroll with the source and pay a fee to them before they release the job info to you. That doesn't mean you get the job; only that they have made money off you by providing you with a lead…and there is no guarantee that the lead is legitimate.

The first piece of advice is simply to do your due diligence on every supplier, especially when you are dealing with suppliers in an online venue and are not able to meet them in person or examine their facilities. When you are engaging in business of this or any other type, there is a certain element of risk involved, and

you must weigh that risk. There may be a time in the future when you will be subject to a con, and you will lose money. But here is what separates entrepreneurs from people who spend their lives punching the time clock: you are willing to take the risk, absorb it when it does happen, and move on.

For the most part, wholesalers who want to tell you that you can get rich quick, make thousands of dollars a week, or obtain high-quality items at an unrealistically low price, are just going to separate you from your money. No one is going to get rich quick on eBay. You may, however, get rich slowly, if you try hard.

Any legitimate wholesaler will provide some information about the company on the website. If a wholesaler does not include contact information, a history of the company, and the names of its officers, give it a pass. If the only contact information is an email address, move on to the next one. You should be able to pick up the phone and talk to a real person before ordering. Even if you do not actually follow through with a phone call, just knowing that the possibility is there will give you a little reassurance.

You can also contact the Consumer Affairs division of the state government where the wholesaler is doing business as well as the local Better Business Bureau. While most of these agencies are "toothless" in being able to take legal action against unscrupulous wholesalers, they (at the least) do keep records of complaints. A simple inquiry into the track record of the wholesaler may give you insight into whether you want to do business with them or find another supplier or even if they are a legitimate business. Always remember to do your "due diligence" before you give away your money.

There are also people out there who will sell you lists of whole-salers and suppliers. You may be tempted to buy one of these lists, because when you are first starting out, you may find it difficult to find legitimate wholesalers who will sell to you in small volumes. However, these lists, for the most part, are often useless and contain very little information above what you could discover on your own. The Internet is a singular creation and the scale of information that can be found on it is amazing. Of course, just as mentioned previously with the directories for drop shippers and closeouts, finding something on the internet doesn't necessarily make it true, so it's crucial to be vigilant about verifying with other eBay businesses and customers how useful and reliable certain databases are.

Chapter 9

Too Much Is Never Enough

o you have what it takes to handle 20 items a day? How about 40 or 100? Your success hinges on logistics. How many can you move, how much are you making on each, and can you get it at a price that will make it worth doing?

After you start selling on eBay, your goal is to turn it into a legitimate, real business. You want it to grow. Sure, it is fun to sell a few odds and ends on eBay, clean out your attic, and make a little spending money, but why limit yourself to earning enough to buy new fridge, when you could earn enough for a new house?

If you are serious about it and put in the time, your eBay business will start growing, sometimes even without your trying too hard. We have all heard the statistics about how many small businesses fail in the first year.

Surprisingly, they do not all fail because of lack of sales. Many businesses fail because they grew too fast and were not logistically equipped to handle the increase. Your current operation may work very well for selling 12 items a week, but when you start moving 100 items a week, those home-made systems start to break down. Your methods of acquiring goods will not necessarily scale up to a bigger business.

Getting Organized

Rummaging around in your basement for old boxes and keeping track of sales in a spiral notebook will not work for long. Larger businesses are constantly streamlining their operations. For successful ones, it is a never-ending process. It should be for you, too.

When you start selling more, if you still use the same procedures you used when you were selling just a few items, you are bound to make mistakes. You can keep track of 4 or 5 sales in your head; you cannot keep track of 100. If you insist on using the same techniques, bad things will almost certainly happen - you will forget shipments, send out the same thing twice, send the wrong item to a customer, and pretty soon, you will start getting negative feedback. Once you get a few of those, your eBay business is toast. Make more than a few mistakes, get a handful of negative reviews, and there is no way to redeem yourself. You are out of business.

Big businesses spend hundreds of thousands of dollars - sometimes millions of dollars - on operational software, techniques, and procedures, and often spend big money to bring in consultants on an ongoing basis to review and refine those processes. If they are involved in shipping out goods, they use technology such as RFID to keep track of inventory and ensure accurate product picking. When a product is picked off the shelf for shipment, the RFID tag is read, and the inventory system is automatically notified. When inventory gets low, the system will automatically place an order for more goods. The same information also goes automatically to a billing application, and the customer account is noted. When that tag is read, data may go simultaneously to six or seven different applications.

You do not need to buy the sophisticated integrated systems used by these huge corporations, but you can take a lesson from them. To start out with, here are a few simple ways to make things easier.

- Pack items as you list them
- Pre return address them
- Label package with item number or part number

- Put them on shelves or file them away so that you can locate them easily
- Enlist help in assembly line operation
- Use an Internet-based postage service and carrier pick-up as opposed to making frequent trips to the post office
- Always make sure that you have a tracking number on each package

Even as a part-time eBay seller, you will be listing at least 10 to 15 auctions a week. Full-time sellers often list upwards of 100 auctions per week.

There are two types of auction management tools: Internet-based, and standalone (non-Internet based). You need to choose which one you need. If you manage your auctions from more than one computer, you need an Internet-based auction management tool. If not, you need a standalone tool.

If you list fewer than five to ten auctions at a single time, you can probably manage them with the old pen and paper method, or by using a simple spreadsheet. Should you choose this method, follow a few simple steps for keeping track of the auctions: use a separate sheet for each auction. Write down the item number, listing date, listing price, category, and comments. Or just use the item number - all the other data is contained within it.

When the auction is over, write down the end date, the sell price, and the buyer's information. Index them by auction number for quick reference. This method works fine for about ten auctions a week.

If you list more than that, you should use a database of some kind, such as Auction Tamer, Auction Wizard 2000, or some other similar software. Selling your merchandise is only half the battle - you must keep track of sales lest you find yourself lost and confused.

It is surprisingly easy to get lost while selling on eBay. You need to keep track of the eBay fees and keep tabs of your profit margin as well as your total income. Even eBay users who sell a great number of items may unknowingly make very little money or run at a loss. It is important for you to periodically check your account records on eBay to insure that you have received credits you were entitled to including refund of listing fees, refunds of sales that were cancelled or otherwise went south, look at what fees are being deducted, etc. Without this periodic review you may find you are making less than you thought.

There are several useful tools to help you keep track of your profits and losses. The profit calculator from www.CalculatorSoup.com (located in the Finance folder) is one of the most popular tools to do this.

Inventory Costs

When deciding on a product or products to offer, after you have considered the market, the competition, and the potential markup, you also have to consider the costs that you will incur that relate to the product. These are some of the so-called "hidden costs" that all retailers face in the form of inventory carrying costs. Besides the wholesale cost you pay for the product, and the eBay listing fees, there are other costs you will face as well, and these costs will be greater or lesser, depending on the product. These costs may include:

- Storage
- Opportunity
- Insurance
- Tracking fees
- Costs of packing materials (this can add up quickly; try to take advantage of free shipping supplies offered by various shippers)

For example, is your product very large? Sure, you may have discovered that there is a market for it, and you may be able to get a decent margin, but there is a cost involved in having to store that huge item until it sells. If you deal in very large products, you will run out of space in your garage quickly and will have to pay for storage or warehousing space. Before listing anything for sale, make sure you have figured out your shipping costs (packaging materials, shipping cost, insurance, tracking fees,

etc.); remember that costs can vary depending on distance from you to your buyer, method of shipping, speed of delivery, etc. Know this in advance so that you can accurately quote shipping costs in your listing. Obviously, you cannot know where your buyer is before a sale is completed; what I like to do is figure out shipping from Florida (where I live) to Seattle, Washington and quote that as an estimate of shipping cost. I also state that the buyer will only be charged actual shipping costs (unless I'm offering free shipping). On items that are simply too big to ship (major appliances, large pieces of furniture, etc.) you may want to list them as "local pickup only". But understand that this will greatly limit your customer base for that item unless your buyer owns a moving company or is willing to hire a mover.

There is also an opportunity cost involved. For example, suppose you obtain a rare and unusual antique and realize that when you sell it, you are very likely to double your money. However, you have already put a great deal of money into it, and the market is such that you may have to hold it for several months before it will sell. That means that you will have that much less money available to buy other products in the meantime. Buying products that will not sell quickly may pay off in the end, but in the short run, it may cost you.

Also, a costly item may require insurance. You will have to insure it for shipping, although you can pass this expense on to your customer. In the meantime, while the valuable item is sitting in your warehouse, you will want to have insurance to cover it against loss, damage, and theft. Most renters and homeowners insurance policies cover personal property, but there are dollar limitations. You should review your insurance policy and see if you need to raise your limits to cover both your own property as well as your business property. You will also have to document your merchandise in the event of a loss. This means you need to have receipts, proof of purchase cost and photographs of your stuff.

You don't need photos of each of the 10,000 widgets you just bought to resell; just take a close-up of one widget and then stand back and photo all the widgets in their shipping crates, boxes, whatever. If you have shelves full of antiques or collectibles, take a picture of the really valuable stuff, along with group shots of the storage shelves so that an adjuster can see there was merchandise on there and not just trash. Periodically retake the photos to keep your photo file current...this depends on how frequently you turn over your merchandise.

Return Receipt and Tracking Information

This is one example of how costs can affect the bottom line.

The one thing that you MUST have on all your sales is a **tracking number on your package**. On packages shipped via U.S. Postal Priority Mail, tracking is included at no additional charge. In the event of a dispute with a buyer, if you don't have tracking confirmation, eBay will uniformly come down on the side of the buyer. This is unfair to honest sellers, but it is a factor of doing business on eBay. EBay even has an online entry where you plug in the tracking number once the package has shipped. This is not only proof of timely shipment by you but it protects the seller against fraudulent buyer claims. Read the terms of the Seller Protection Program on eBay as well as the Buyer Protection

Program. You will note that eBay offers better protection to buyers than it does to its sellers. This is something that has slowly evolved over the past 5-10 years and may account for why many sellers stopped using eBay and switched to alternative Internet selling sites. As a seller, I have had several bad experiences where eBay sided with the buyer who was obviously engaging in fraudulent conduct, simply because I as seller had not fully complied with eBay's requirements.

The U.S. Postal Service also offers Return Receipt, a service that is easy to use and eliminates buyer fraud. The post office gives you a confirmation by mail or email that your package was delivered and who signed for it. Sometimes, something like this is necessary - there are people out there who will try to cheat you and say that they never received their package, when in fact they really did. If you have Return Receipt, you can prove they received it.

Is it worthwhile to use Return Receipt on every single shipment? Probably not. It is yet another expense and the small expenses add up and can eventually kill a business if you're not mindful about them. Your margins may be very low to begin with because of the extremely high competition

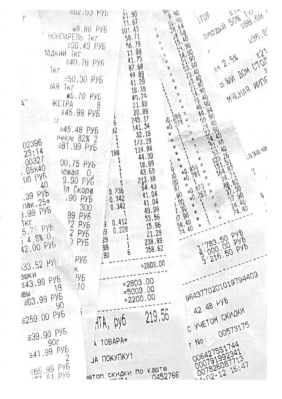

on eBay, and the money spent on delivery confirmation and other fulfillment expenses can easily turn profit into loss. The thing to do is to examine your loss rate, and look at the value of the items you are shipping.

Now here comes the part where you really need to just sit down and do the math yourself so you can verify the worth of using Return Receipts on all of your shipments. First, take the value of Return Receipt, or $1.35. Now, figure your loss rate. Let's say for the sake of argument that 1 in 100 packages gets lost. (In reality, the loss rate is not likely to be anywhere near that high.) If you provide Return Receipt for 100 packages, then you have spent $135. Now figure the average value of shipments. Let's say again for the sake of argument that it is $25. Now your Return Receipt will allow you to avoid taking a loss on the $25 value of the lost package, but you have spent $135 for the privilege - and have lost $110 in the process. It would have been cheaper, therefore, not to use Return Receipt, just take the $25 loss, and replace the product without any argument.

On the other hand, suppose the value of your shipments is higher. Assuming a 1 in 100 loss rate and $1.35 for Return Receipt, the break-even point at which it becomes profitable to use the service would be $135 per shipment. Therefore, in this example, if your shipments average less than $135 in value, you should not use Return Receipt; if average value is greater than $135, you should.

Chapter 10

Finding Your Niche – Begin at the End

Many eBay users have been searching for that "perfect" item to sell - the Holy Grail of the online auction world. Like most of you, we are still looking. The fact is, there is no "perfect" item, and even if you do find one that comes close to perfection, your success with it may only last so long until other sellers cut into your action or the item becomes passé. Nonetheless, we have discovered some very interesting items while continuing our quest.

Choosing the best products to sell involves a lot more than finding something you think people would like to buy. To be sure you have to think of everything else that affects that bid: what it will cost to ship the package, what kind of packing materials you will need, and whether you will need to insure the package. There may well be someone out there who will want to buy the 1,000-pound antique glass sculpture, but how in the world are you going to wrap it, protect it, and ship it? Think backwards. Think of shipping costs, weight, availability of packaging, and choose a product that is certain to yield a profit.

If you pay $1 or $2 for an item that goes for $3 or $4, and you charge the correct amount for shipping, you have done well. Extremely fragile items that require special packaging may sell for a good price on the auction market, but when it comes time to put it in a box and send it out, that extra packaging and insurance can eat up your profit. And you do not want to gouge your customer on the shipping to recoup a loss.

Here are some tips before you lock into one item to call your own. Look first to your hobbies and interests, as the most successful pitch is always from your own heart. It may sound trite, but it is nonetheless true. If you do not believe in what you are selling, your online business is doomed. Never sell an item you are not at least a little excited about – even if your excitement comes from the potential profit; otherwise, you had better be able to fake it like a Hollywood actor.

Checklist of Things to Do
Before Choosing Merchandise

❑ I have made a list of subjects I am proficient in or have special knowledge about

❑ I have done my due diligence to determine if the things I know about are being purchased regularly on eBay and how many people are selling them

❑ I have considered how much space I have for storage of inventory

❑ I have considered alternatives such as drop shipping arrangements with suppliers that will reduce my need for storage of inventory

❑ I have compiled a list of area manufacturers and distributors who may be sources of products

❑ I have considered purchasing new or used items locally (rummage sales, estate sales, auctions, etc.) and decided whether I will use these as a source

❑ If I plan to create custom products, I am aware of all copyright laws and how they may or may not apply to the items I am making

You have devoted thought to identifying your product and have completed the "getting started" phase. You are excited about your choices and are ready to begin selling them on eBay auctions. The next step is to identify your category.

Considering that eBay has over 1,000 categories, this should be a relatively simple process, but there is one important thing to know: before posting your item in a category, follow these steps.

First, browse through the various eBay categories and jot down the ones you feel relate to your product. You should be able to identify five to ten possible candidates.

Look at other sales of similar items to yours…what categories are they listed under?

Check List

- ☑ ....
- ☐ ....
- ☐ ....
- ☐ ....
- ☐ ....
- ☐ ....

Next, record the number of auctions currently listed in each of those categories. The number of current auctions appears beside the category name.

An average in most categories is around 1,000, so if you see more than 1,000, you may safely conclude that the category is fairly active, and if you see less than 1,000 it is relatively speaking, inactive.

Categories with upwards of 3,000 auctions are very popular and those few with 10,000 are certainly the most popular. By using this ranking system, you can then rate the categories for your chosen product.

Choose active categories because they see the most traffic. If you list your product in a relatively inactive area, you may get few or even no bids, even if you feature your item. Therefore, avoid categories with fewer than 1,000 auctions.

The first category is free. For an additional fee, you can list your item in more than one category. The value of this is questionable however; many buyers simply look for their key words under "all categories" and do not limit it to specific categories.

One other tip for your listing…if a word has alternate spellings, intentionally use the different variations within the listing description. A search will then turn up your listing even if spelled incorrectly by a potential buyer. For example, Hallicrafters is a well-known vintage manufacturer of military and amateur radio equipment from the 1930s through the 1970s. It is often misspelled as Halicrafter, Halicrafters, etc. If you have a Hallicrafters radio to sell, by using the different spellings in your description you may be found by a potential buyer who misspelled the name. For buyers, this can be a good way of finding a hidden auction not getting a lot of attention because the Seller listed the misspelled name in his title without realizing his error.

Settling on your category is a clue to your "niche." The definition means that you will have little or no competition from other sellers, so you can corner your market. You will become a certified guru of the items you sell as you ideally be the only one on eBay offering the products. You can see why finding your niche is critical to your success.

Your expertise will make it much easier to spot bargains as you shop for products to resell. Bargains might be all around you, but if you know nothing about the products, you will not recognize them.

You will find different ways to add personal value to your products. These low cost add-ons or unique twists to your products will drastically increase your sales and profits by making your items more desirable.

By dealing with the same type of customer over a long period, you will come to understand what your customer wants. You will sell your products better and market them in new ways.

You will be knowledgeable and enthusiastic about what you sell, and you will be attentive to your customer's desires. Satisfied customers and name recognition mean repeat business.

With passion for what you are doing, you have a much greater chance of sticking to it and loving it. It will not even feel like work. It will be as if you are being paid to play.

> I have found all the products I sell to be successful because I found my niche a long time ago when I started selling products that I personally love (ladies fashions and handbags)! This way you become an expert in your own field.

Have you ever collected anything? What do you like to read? What do you do in your spare time? Do you have a favorite pastime? What was your major in college? What jobs have you had? Are there any other fields where you have a great amount of knowledge? What clubs' or organizations' meetings do you attend? Can you think of novel ideas that people who share your passion would love? Make a list of your hobbies and interests or things you have always wanted to know more about. List what you are passionate about.

Study the category listings on eBay to get additional ideas for products you can turn into an eBay business. Consider how you can turn your expertise into a product and how you can add value to current products related to your interests. For example, if you make or collect trout lures, consider these interests and hobbies relating to it: hunting, fishing, camping, hiking, boating, and lure collecting. EBay attracts buyers who collect things relating to their hobbies and interests, and chances are, you can bring a new twist or angle to selling items related to your interests.

List all possible products that you can sell that may be one of a kind and have little or no competition.

Through research and trial and error, I eventually found my niche. I sell photography lighting equipment and tools to help other eBay users. The key is to know your market. The products must be available at a larger than average discount while also having a steady demand. Identifying such merchandise requires many hours of research and, sometimes, even months of effort. You must monitor your sales closely to determine exactly what sells at a healthy profit. But when you find your niche, a steady income will be your reward.

Rome Was Not Built in a Day

Sometimes it is not enough merely to have something to sell. If your only goal is to hold a garage sale on eBay and turn your old junk into quick cash, eBay is a no-brainer. List stuff you are not using anyway, get paid, and smile all the way to the bank.

As a venue for selling old stuff you have stored in your attic, it can be wonderful, so long as you do not have high expectations. But then again, if it is just sitting in your attic anyway, if you make $10 or $20, you are still ahead of the game.

However, if you want to have an eBay business, that is simply not enough. You have to have a different approach, and you naturally will have higher expectations for your earnings. If you plan to turn eBay into a small business, a supplemental income, or even an occupation, you are going to have to be much more careful about what you buy.

It *is* true that nearly everything will sell on eBay, or at least, there is someone trying to sell it at any given point in time. It is also true, however, that many things on eBay typically sell at well *below* retail value because of eBay's nature as a near-ideal market: every seller can approach every buyer at the same time with no barriers, real or imagined, to trade. EBay is a buyers' market. If you want to buy something, chances are, there are a hundred people selling it, and you can pick and choose and find the absolute lowest price. It is possible, however, to make money in a buyers' market, and the trick is in being extremely careful about the items you select for sale.

For manufactured goods that are neither rare nor out of production, this potential for near-infinite supply has the effect of driving prices down. EBay is no place to sell basic, commodity goods that can be found in every department store in every town in America. To be sure, those types of products can be found on eBay, and if you are looking to buy, you can get a deal. But to sell them, you need to buy a huge quantity at a great price.

Fads and Trends

At the same time, the rapidity with which stock can enter and leave the supply chain on eBay leads to a marketplace in which demand can fluctuate as rapidly as consumer tastes. If you are a seller who has invested real money in your inventory with the expectation of generating a return, you do not want to be caught suddenly with worthless stock! You may, for example, find that a certain item has sold well and place an order for a thousand of them. However, by the time you have sold your first 100 or so,

demand changes, and they start turning up at discount department stores and dollar stores, and you are stuck with goods you
cannot sell.

As anyone with children knows very well, there are certain items
that for a brief time are a "must-have." Certain types of toys, collectibles, or trading cards go in and out of fashion quickly and
represent a tremendous opportunity for profit.

Fad items can be an excellent short-term profit-maker, but be
very aware that it is extremely short-term. If you buy too many,
you may just get stuck with a garage full of something no one
wants any more. Do you remember Beanie Babies? They are cute,
and you can still find them and collect them, but for a short time,
they were a huge fad. Certain ones were selling for top dollar,
sometimes in excess of a $100. Today, you can buy them from flea
marketers for $2 or $3 each. While they may be fun to collect, they
have little value.

The best way to approach these sorts of fad items is to buy them
in small enough quantities that you can move your inventory
quickly and not get left with too much when they lose their steam.

Cross-Sell Items

In selecting your product line, take into account the cross-sell.
This simply means offering products that go with other products.
This is a simple, easy way to expand your inventory, and get ad-
ditional sales from your existing customers.

It is a simple concept. If you sell cellular telephones, for example, you can also offer cell phone cases, decorative facades for cell phones, cell phone accessories like chargers, headphones, and a host of other products that people may want to go along with their phone.

Similarly, if you offer something mechanical or that has parts that may wear out, offer the replaceable parts as well.

Types of Goods

If you look around eBay and you will see just about everything you could possibly imagine. Look closer and you will see that many of them are receiving no bids. Say for example, you get a deal on some wholesale tableware sets. But before you place your order for a thousand, take a look at your local Kmart, Big Lots, Wal-Mart, Target, etc. Tableware sets there cost as little as $10, and it is not likely that people will be looking on eBay for them unless they are extremely special, custom-made, or very unusual. Find a set of silverware that was once used by the King of Siam, and you have a good eBay item. The same set on sale at Kmart for $10? Now you are wasting your eBay fees.

Yet there are people making lots of money on eBay and making hundreds of sales weekly.

Those are the folks who are trafficking in the right types of merchandise.

Chapter 11

Your Strategy

O ne of the keys to reaping huge profits on eBay is to develop an efficient strategy before you list your item. You need to know what type of product you want to list, what your niche market is on eBay, and have a profile you have created about your typical customer. Additionally, you should already have decided which categories are best for your item.

You are now ready to establish the strategy for your business. Keep in mind however, that as any good military man knows, it is NOT about strategy, it is about logistics, but more on that later.

There are two basic types of sellers on eBay: high volume and low volume. High volume sellers are those who list more than ten auctions online at a time. Low volume sellers list fewer than ten auctions at a time. The profit margin of your product often determines which category of seller you are. For example, if you sell real estate and you make $10,000 per sale, you may need only list a few properties per week to make a fortune. The same applies to the sale of jewelry, cars, and most other items that have a large profit margin. However, if you sell inexpensive items, you may only make $5 to $10 per sale. In that case, you will need to list hundreds of items at once in order to make big profits, and thus you would be a high volume seller.

Why would someone go through the effort and hassle of listing so many individual items when it is so easy to list a few larger ones and make a fortune? The answer goes to the essence of Internet sales: most online buyers spend only $50 or less for a product.

Another reason high volume sellers are more numerous and will often make more money on eBay, even though their products cost less, is that it is relatively easy to purchase inexpensive items in bulk at wholesale prices, but it is often very difficult to buy big-ticket items such as real estate or automobiles at anything near wholesale. Big-ticket items will yield a smaller margin.

Now that you are armed with this critical information, you need to consider the item you are selling and then make an informed decision on whether to be a high volume or low volume seller. If you have sufficient free time to devote to your online business, we recommend that you go for the high volume seller option. However, if you are a part-time eBay seller, you may wish to begin as a low volume seller, at least until your business begins to take off.

Only you know which option is right for you, based upon the amount of available time and the markup of your merchandise. After you determine which you will be, you are halfway to developing an effective sales strategy on eBay.

The next step in our process is to integrate everything you have learned thus far and project your eBay strategy into the future. For example, we will assume you decide to sell jewelry. Here is a test case for your careful consideration: You have already identified your niche market and have located the related categories. You also know that your buyers will probably spend around $50 to $100 per purchase, and you know that the average profit on your auctions will be around $60.

You have plenty of available time and your profit margin is relatively low, so you then determine you will be a high volume seller and decide to list about 100 to 200 auctions a week. You estimate that about 70 percent of your auctions will end with at least one winning bid, which is the historical eBay average. Based upon this projection, you then calculate your weekly eBay income as $6,300. You plan to keep close tabs on your auctions and discontinue unpopular items and focus on the others.

You have an account already set up with your wholesale jewelry supplier and have invested in enough inventory to supply your first week of sales. Your plan is to re-list every auction as soon as it ends, place your weekly replenishment order for your inventory, and send one weekly mailing to your customers. Your basic sales strategy is established, and you are now ready to list your auctions.

Before you begin, you may want to project your sales strategy as far into the future as you can, run through a series of potential problems, and resolve them. You may wish to write out a paragraph much like the one outlined above and then analyze it. The idea is to know your strategy before you proceed.

We strongly urge that you make all your listings regular auctions in the early going. At this early stage, do not make them Featured Auctions or Dutch Auctions (multiple item listing). Test your sales strategy and then evaluate the viability of your product within its niche market for a few weeks before continuing.

Chapter 12

Finding and Selling Limited-Life Goods

here are four major categories of goods that are the most
viable foundations for eBay businesses:

- limited-life goods
- general goods
- seasonal items
- investment or collectible items

Each of these has its own demand characteristics and is suited to
a particular size, type, and temperament of seller.

Limited lifetime goods are simply what the term sounds like. They are types of goods that are expected to have a limited market demand. They will go through a cycle of demand and supply. There will be a period initially where the price is higher and they are available only at certain retail outlets, but later the price will go down and they can be found in several other places, including secondary markets like eBay. A few excellent examples of limited lifetime goods are:

- Laptops
- TVs
- iPods and MP3 players
- Smart Phones (especially older models)
- Some clothing and accessories
- Current movie or television merchandising goods

How Demand Works – In Brief

- Absolute demand is limited to the early life cycle of the product, but due to low supply before and at the time of product launch (combined with strong marketing efforts from well-financed manufacturers and retailers) even limited demand among early adopters can drive prices very high.

- Demand increases steadily, but supply tends to increase even faster as the market sees opportunities to move product, and production ramps. This drives prices gradually downward as the supply gets greater.

- Inevitably, the product will become obsolete, replaced by something better, or people will just start to lose interest. When the product reaches this end-of-life stage, liquidation stock starts to enter the market in large quantities just as demand drops off in anticipation of the next product or fad, causing prices to fall swiftly in the flash of an eye - not years or months but weeks or even days. The product then starts to show up in discount and outlet stores, and on online venues such as eBay.

Understanding the Market and Pitfalls to Avoid

Limited lifetime goods live in the world of product cycles in one way or another, meaning that the current incarnation of the product is only valuable until the next fad comes along. At that point, it becomes the target of bargain-hunters.

The key to selling in this area of the market is timing, which makes it a precarious way to sell. Nonetheless, there is money in limited lifetime goods both at the beginning and at the end of the product's cycle.

Though these issues also arise in brick-and-mortar inventory management, you must remember that to be early on eBay you have to be *earliest in the world*, and when you liquidate, you are not selling off to a constrained market, but to a single global market in which *the entire worldwide stock for this product* is simultaneously on offer. Can you compete? If you are not sure, limit your investment in the product.

Selling Early

When looking for resources, you will pay much more for your product early on in the product cycle, but if your sources can get you a salable product with a window of opportunity before it is available to the general marketplace, you can make some of the highest margins possible on eBay. Similarly, if in the early stages of release the product is in short supply and high demand and you can obtain the products even at retail cost, you have a good chance of turning a profit.

For example, witness the pre-release sales of game consoles like the XBox on eBay. Sellers who got them before or at release enjoyed a one-to-two week window during which they could sell the items for two or three times their value in a few weeks as supply increases.

Selling on Time

Do not worry if you do not have the ability to find a source of products before the rest of the market. Doing so is often very difficult and you are not alone. You have to be an insider to get a product before major retailers get their hands on it. If you cannot, you will compete with everyone else. In this situation, you are operating much more like a traditional business. Your margin comes from efficiency, good resource relationships or deals, and volume discounts. The window is small when you can actually do that. If you have the funds available and you are able to move products in lots, you can get the volume discounts, but if you are not able to move lots quickly, you are very likely to be stuck with warehouse full of product as the selling cycle dwindles.

Selling End-of-Cycle

If you are a gambler (which you must be to some degree if you want to be a real entrepreneur), this may be an ideal place of entry for you. End-of-cycle selling is tricky, risky, and timing-intensive, but it is better suited to sellers with smaller budgets. Your goal here is to buy product in volume just as the product hits liquidation channels but before demand has dried up as the result of market saturation or the public's anticipation of the replacement product. There *is* usually a window, but you *must* be critical and smart. Are you really ahead of the market and can you really buy liquidation stock *early* and *cheap*? If so, you can make money by buying at liquidation prices and selling at near-retail prices.

Beware, though, that during this part of the cycle, demand is not increasing. At best, it has not yet started to drop, but by pushing this additional liquidation supply into the market, you and your competitors will cause it to drop along with prices. If you buy too late, too high, or too much, you will lose your investment, as this type of stock typically loses more than 90 percent of its value as the next product cycle begins in earnest.

Chapter 13

Finding and Selling General Goods

The "general store" used to be a fixture in small towns across America. Today, selling general goods in small volume is more difficult than it once was, simply because much larger stores carry things in larger quantity, greater variety, and at lower cost. The general store is, for the most part, a thing of the past.

How Demand Works - In Brief

- There are still product cycles in general goods, but they tend to be much longer, and the drop in demand at their end is not so rapid, usually tapering off over months or years, rather than overnight.

- Demand is constrained almost entirely by supply. The more there are on eBay of any one type of item, the less each listing of that type will generate in revenue.

- Used, recycled, and refurbished goods are important components of this marketplace. With longer product cycles and stable pricing, many consumers will buy on price alone.

Understanding the Market and Pitfalls to Avoid

Of all the types of goods you can buy and sell on eBay, general goods present the greatest challenge. Nonetheless, you can build a good eBay business with this type of goods if you have the right strategy.

The challenge with trying to sell general goods on eBay is that these types of products are widely available elsewhere. They tend to be commodity items, where brand name is not always as important. A hammer, after all, is just a shaped piece of metal attached to a stick. What does it matter who manufactures it? Because of the broad availability and ubiquity of these types of items, the price tends to drift to its lowest level.

You are not going to make money on eBay with a business selling general goods at the same price people can find it at their local Wal-Mart. Your challenge here is to try to find these goods at the most attractive rate and sell them lower than department stores. An example is computer printers. They are available everywhere and at low cost, and sometimes you can even get one free when you buy a new computer. Inkjet printers have become commodity items over the years, and there is no great advantage that any one name brand has over another. As a result, they can be had

very easily and cheaply. Still, you can find them on eBay, and there are sellers making good money on them. Here is an example: suppose you want to set up a business selling Inkjet printers on eBay. You know that anyone can go to their local office supply chain store and buy one for $50, so you know that you have to offer them for less than that. Your target audience is not going to be people who want brand new, name-brand printers; rather, they will be bargain hunters who want to pick one up for half the store's price. As such, you will offer two types of printers: 1) used and 2) new no-name printers that you found at an attractive price. The secondary market for bulk Inkjet printers is such that you can probably find a source where you can get them for next to nothing. With a little cleaning up and testing, you can probably turn them around very quickly and sell them for $10 to $25 each with no problem.

It is here that you can become success the old-fashioned way, through hard work, frugality, good customer service, and generally sound business practices. While selling general goods has become the domain of large retailers, you can carve out an attractive niche in this sub-market and make excellent money.

This also ignores many of the reasons that people give for wanting to be eBay sellers, including the ability to achieve massive profits by timing the market or leveraging exclusive relationships, or the possibility of rags-to-riches business models in which a single buy-and-turnaround nets millions. These instant wealth stories *are* true, but there are many failures for every success. This is the type of eBay business that will build slowly and provide you with a steady supply of business over time.

If you are just an honest, common sense businessperson looking for a way to migrate your operation to the 21st Century through eBay, your ticket is a general, consumable goods. Buy frugally with an eye toward quality, stay away from limited-life items, work hard, provide good customer service, and be patient. You will grow and prosper - slowly.

Do Not Try to Do It Fast!

EBay has a tendency to create problems for sellers who want to grow too quickly. Remember that every market - even eBay - is of limited size. Too often a seller who has found a niche is lured by the physically unconstrained and global nature of eBay's selling space to over-list or oversell in a market. The truth is that eBay does not scale linearly forever. Buy too much stock and post too many listings at once and you will find that you have driven your own price down thanks to oversupply.

A seller doing fine at 50 listings a month might find that with 200 listings a month supply has exceeded demand and his auctions are now competing against themselves. Not only do items end up selling for less than they were selling for before, but a percentage of the items are now also going unsold entirely, causing revenue to plummet because of listing fees and overhead.

Diversify

Sellers in this market also need to be aware of the unending possibility for new competition to arise. Remember that on eBay all sellers share the same floor space - there is no way to corner a local market on anything. One of the greatest things about eBay, and about Internet commerce in general, is the low barrier to entry. You do not have to put out money to open up a physical shop; anyone with a computer can make a website and start selling something. However, while that is one of the most attractive things there is about Internet commerce, it is also one of the greatest obstacles. Because anyone can play, it means you will have more competition.

When you do well selling something, inevitably someone will see your success and try to duplicate it. By diversifying your sales, you hedge against the possibility that you will lose half your revenue in a flash the moment another seller decides to move onto your turf.

There is money in general merchandise and consumables on eBay, but you must remain flexible and light-footed to make it work. To rely on any one relationship or type of product indefinitely means failure inevitably.

Chapter 14

Finding and Selling Seasonal Items

very Christmas season, we hear people complaining about how early the stores start putting out their Christmas items for sale, but the cycle continues. Traditionally, the day after Thanksgiving was the first day of Christmas shopping; today, Christmas decorations start appearing in department stores before Halloween and even after Labor Day!

Similarly, for those of us who live in places where there are seasonal changes in weather, we have to time our purchases of winter and summer clothing. Have you ever tried to buy a good short-sleeved shirt in the fall? It cannot be done in most states. The only place you can find one is in the close-out section, after all the good ones have already been picked through. Some good examples of seasonal items include:

- Holiday decorations
- Recreational equipment
- Weather-specific apparel

Seasonal items tend to be less generalized. Every year we always are on the lookout for that special Christmas decoration to grace our tree. We want something new and different, something that no one has ever seen before, that will wow and awe our Christmas guests.

How Demand Works - In Brief

- Both supply and demand reach peak *before* the season in question - for natural seasons, generally in the preceding quarter; for holiday seasons, generally in the leading two months.

- Demand begins to decline in advance of supply once the season is reached, gradually driving prices downward and leading into eventual liquidation.

- Liquidation occurs during the period immediately following the season and demand is low, limited primarily to those looking for good deals in anticipation of the season's return next year. If the goods are not time-limited, liquidation stops once the overhead of maintaining the goods becomes less than the losses incurred by liquidating them now in the face of waning demand.

Sourcing and selling seasonal goods is always a little different from any other type of product. Source the goods well in advance of the season - or alternately, just after the season ends and save them for next year. Ever been at the grocery store the day after Halloween? Half price candy! What a deal. Of course, the candy will not keep for a year, but some items will. You can pick up excellent quality, non-perishable, seasonal items after the season is over, not only from your regular wholesale sources, but even from regular retail outlets liquidating their seasonal stock. Of course, the drawback is that you will have to have the storage space to keep these goods until the next season begins, but when it does, you will have the goods on hand that you have picked up at bargain-basement prices.

Understanding the Market and Pitfalls to Avoid

It is no shock that Christmas items do not sell well in January or that bikinis have a limited appeal when it is ten below zero. But as an eBay seller, you are on the opposite side of that fence. January may well be the best time to buy your Christmas seasonal items in anticipation of the next selling period. By the same token, when it starts snowing and department stores sell off their remaining stock of bikinis at a discount that would be a good opportunity to find some deals. Offering items in the off-season has its advantages, too. Consider, for example, how likely is a Minnesotan to find cruise wear locally in mid-winter?

The trick to success with these goods is to buy those that will retain their value across annual cycles so that overstock does not become worthless if you cannot move it all in time. That is why after Halloween is over that Halloween candy starts going at 75 percent off or even more - they cannot keep it until next Halloween, and if they do not sell it soon, it will become worthless. It is also clear that the best

time to buy is on the opposite ebb of the annual cycle, essentially two quarters ahead, when prices are at liquidation levels.

I sell holiday goods that fit my general criteria:
1. Profitable.
2. Easy to Ship.
3. Limited liability (not fragile or controversial).

A buying tactic available to small sellers is the "early order" program many suppliers have. The Christmas season is a prime example. Many distributors will discount merchandise and give you longer payment terms, say 90 days, if you place your Christmas order months in advance (sometimes as early as January or February) and agree to have it delivered in August or September. It is a win-win for both parties. The supplier gets an idea for how much inventory to bring in, and the eBay seller gets a discount for early ordering.

If you buy later to get "this year's" goods, be alert about whether you are buying limited-life goods that will have to be sold this year. Beware, too, that you will face direct competition from those still selling last year's goods, picked up at liquidation prices in anticipation of this year's season.

Check out the "end of season" sales that the local retailers have. Stock up on end-of-summer sales items and sell them at peak time in the spring. Then stock up on winter stuff at the end of winter and start selling them at peak time in the fall.

If you have an eBay store, sell these items year round and consider selling internationally as these buyers will buy your product year round.

Keep up with what your local retailers are doing and when they are doing it. Doing this will help you decide when the time is right for certain products to be launched.

Timing the Seasonal Goods Market

The demand curve for seasonal goods is similar to the one for limited-life goods, but there is largely no early adopter premium: except in very specific cases, there is little benefit to buying goods high early in hopes of being able to sell them to irrationally eager early adopters.

If the value of your resource deals is primarily in product quality, brand, or other non-price metrics, the best time to hit the market is just *before* the listing glut that will drive prices down. If you can be the one to convince buyers to shop for an upcoming season before the other sellers begin to list, you will stay ahead of the demand curve and your stock will enjoy some of the best pricing of the season.

If the value of your resource deals is primarily in low price, the best time to hit the market is during the seasonal buying boom when your low buy-ins mean that you can undersell your competitors just when consumers are doing seasonal shopping in the greatest numbers.

Chapter 15

Collectibles, Pickers, and Auctions

ollectibles represent one of the biggest opportunities on eBay. People who collect unusual items will look everywhere they can to find that one piece they need to complete their collection, and they resort to eBay very often to find that perfect little item for their mantel.

The great advantage to dealing in this type of goods is that the demand for a particular collectible can be very high - much higher than any other type of product. You also have the possibility of finding collectible goods at very low prices and selling them at many times your cost. This is the only category where it would be possible to find something for a dollar and sell it for a thousand. Some examples of collectible and investment items include:

- Antiques
- Keepsake clocks and timepieces
- Fine jewelry
- Baseball cards, comic books, and figures

When trying to find a source for these types of goods, you will be in a different boat. Unlike general commodity goods that you can get from any one of a thousand wholesalers or drop shippers, collectibles are usually one-of-a-kind items. Your sources will tend to be smaller shops and other collectors and individuals who do not realize the value of what they have. If you are dealing in antiques, for example, there is no big wholesale antique warehouse you go to

for your product. You will get your products from individuals, yard sales, thrift shops, and estate sales. Unlike other types of products, where you can set up a relationship with a supplier to provide you with a constant flow of products, antiques and collectible dealers are constantly on the hunt for things to sell.

> As an eBay consignment seller who sells for others, I have found a new passion for antiques and vintage items. This is definitely a gold mine on eBay. Past eBay students of mine have attended storage unit sales and have landed wonderful resalable items. Estate sales can be very rewarding, too.

How Demand Works - In Brief

- Demand in these markets depends on two things: limited supply and expert sentiment, for which many euphemisms exist - public opinion, market regard, preferences of a collecting or investing "community," and conventional wisdom.

- Watch out for unexpected supply gluts of the kind that can occur when a major player's assets are liquidated or sold off, as this can cause the bottom to drop out of a market with little or no notice.

- Demand for collectible goods is unpredictable, and defies the logic usually applied to demand economics in any other type of commercial environment. The value is all about perception. A baseball, for example, may be worth only $2, but if it is signed by Babe Ruth, it is worth whatever anyone wants to pay for it. The value of many collectibles and antiques does go up dramatically over time, and many people see them as not only a fun hobby, but also as an investment. The value also goes down, especially during an economic recession. We have seen that in the past few years...collectibles which sold for thousands are now worth less than $100. Obviously, certain collectibles never lose their value, but the challenge is finding those collectibles and recognizing them for what they are.

- It helps to have some knowledge of the product category you are dealing in. If you are selling antique Chinese vases, you must have some knowledge of Chinese history and art and be able to tell the real thing from a fake. You have to be able to tell your customer where it came from, when it was made, and a little bit about the history of it. Items with anecdotes about their owners or their part in history convey pride of ownership or intrinsic value that translates into real money.

- Several factors determine the value and price of the product you are selling. With other goods, you simply may be able to do some cost accounting and come up with a workable profit margin. That does not work with antiques. Of course, you want to make a profit, but the markup can be many times your cost in some cases, depending on the perceived value of the item.

- If you are selling consumer electronics, for example, the market may determine that you can have a markup of about 15 percent, and that is it. However, the markup on that 17th Century painting you found at a yard sale for a dollar last week may be thousands of percent.

- Besides perceived value, the scarcity of the product will also go into the price determination, as well as the reputation of the maker (manufacturer or artist), desirability, and the value that has accrued over the years or decades. The other demand sphere fluctuates rapidly and comes from collecting or investing "fads," usually at the hands of the media or experts (often with vested interests). You need genuine expertise or a flair for floating above the ebb and tide of collector fads to leverage the fluctuations for profit.

Understanding the Market and Pitfalls to Avoid

Naturally, finding resources in these markets is largely a matter of luck, insider information, expertise, and long-standing relationships. Generally speaking, these are difficult and risky markets to enter if you do not already have a passion for and knowledge of the market in question, beyond the desire to buy and sell. Excellent fake copies of antiquities in bazaars in Asia sell for the equivalent of about $10, when the real thing may cost thousands. If you have the knowledge about these sorts of items, an eye for quality and collectability, and can tell the real thing when you see it, you may do very well.

These are also much slower markets, with limited room for sellers that will make a good living exclusively trading in them and nowhere else. There may be a category of antique that is so unusual that only a handful of people in the world sell them. If you are lucky enough to have a connection or two, and you can get your hands on a regular supply of them, then you may be in for a good run. Keep in mind though, that if there are only a handful of people in the world selling them, there may also only be a handful of people buying them.

In some cases, even if there are few buyers, they may be willing to pay almost anything for what they want. They place a heavy premium on relationships and reputation, both of which are slow to build, and shifting product is often a much slower process. Supply is very limited, but so is demand, often to just one or two

people in the world. Even if they are saving up specifically to buy the item that *you* want to sell them, there is no revenue in it for you until someone who wants the item actually **has the money to buy it**.

To summarize, consistent income in this eBay market depends on a myriad of factors, many of them requiring a solid foundation of product experience:

- Both breadth and depth in inventory

- Multiple sales channels (eBay alone is unlikely to suffice)

- Absolute dedication to quality and customer service

- Personality or personalities amenable to a business that trades in relationships and individual amiability/reputation

- Enough knowledge of the product to separate the wheat from the chaff at an expert level; fakes and fraudulent goods can be rampant here

- Enough knowledge of the marketplace to separate fads from real value and to spot coming shifts, for example, from unexpected dumping of previously rare goods

This is probably the toughest market to break into and one of the hardest to enter when building a business around eBay sales. If you dedicate yourself to becoming an expert in one aspect of this market, the more likely your success, particularly if the product is available, collectible, and shippable, and has some value, such as Depression glass, cut glass, or blown glass.

You can start your study with a library book on collectibles and visits to antique stores.

The higher your level of expertise the lower your risk. If you are already a major player or expert, there is relatively little risk to you if you have sound business sense and good customer service. If you are a newcomer to the market, the risk is very high, since you do not yet know how much you do not know. If you cannot authenticate an antique, you could lose everything in the acquisition phase before you even get started.

For example, Lionel Tin Plate Trains is the description for stamped tin or steel toy trains manufactured by Lionel from around 1903 until just after World War II, when die casting became the preferred manufacturing choice. These trains (individual cars and complete sets) can be worth thousands of dollars or just be good for restoration parts (a few bucks) depending on:

- Scarcity (how many were manufactured and how many are known to still exist)

- Condition (any parts missing? Are all the parts original? Are there dents, rust, etc.?)

- Original Finish (watch out for repainting and touch-ups)

- Restoration (was the item restored at any time or is it factory original)

- Does it include the original box and all packing materials, instruction sheets, etc.?

With some individual pieces, they are so rare that some of the above considerations may not even have any effect on the value of the piece, but you have to know which pieces those are and what to look for. Dealing in such items can be extremely hazardous to your financial health unless you are experienced and knowledgeable in this field.

Of all the markets or types of goods you can choose to build your business around, however, the investment or collectible goods market is the most satisfying to its sellers.

Who Are Pickers?

Picking refers to the practice of buying antiques at auctions, sales, and private parties, and then reselling them. Re-sales used to be limited to antique shops, but no longer, due to the popularity of programs on the History Channel and other cable networks. Folks who do this are known as "pickers." They perform a unique function in the antique business.

These folks sell to dealers, decorators, antiques collectors, and private individuals with whom they have an ongoing relationship. In other words, a picker develops sources for goods. They may even have their own retail or online business.

A dealer who sells merchandise at lower prices to other dealers is not always a picker; a dealer who sells her items at a low price is not always a wholesaler.

These resourceful scavengers scour auctions, estate sales, newspaper ads, and flea markets for items they can sell to antique shops and dealers, and they are on a perpetual treasure hunt, making them good people for an eBay seller to know since they do the legwork. A picker is usually someone with another income, such as a retiree, preferably with storage space, a truck or a van, a nose for a bargain, and an addiction for treasure hunting. If you know one, you can intercept his sale to an antique store and increase your profit on the resale. If you are one, eBay will save you time and money and open your wondrous finds to a wide audience of buyers.

Most wholesalers tend to be broad based generalists - they trade in any item on which they can make a profit. Pickers, in contrast, tend more often to be specialists who buy a few types of merchandise and service a limited clientele. Many pickers specialize in one small area, such as rare and antique books. They know who their customers are and what types of things they may be looking for. If for example, you trade in antique Japanese swords, they will be looking out for them as they go from place to place. If they are good, they will know your business as well as you do yourself, and will have a good feel for the type of products you want, specific details, and how much you would be willing to pay.

To reduce selling expenses to almost nothing, an astute whole-saler - who is willing to sell decent quality items at less than retail - can quite literally make a greater profit on those items than can a retail dealer on that exact item.

Wholesale dealers and pickers who slight their regular custom-ers by denying access to some of their finest items, so they can be sold at retail shows and auctions, make substantial profit in the short-term but ultimately lose in the longer term simply because their customer base evaporates. The best picker will establish a close, ongoing relationship with you. Ultimately, they will make their money by helping you make money as well.

It literally takes years for a wholesale dealer or a picker to garner a significant following. It takes tremendous work every year to maintain that clientele and to compensate for buyers lost due to retirement. When a wholesale dealer or a picker sells an item to someone who is not on his client list, that person is for all intents and purposes no longer a wholesaler.

A smart picker will sell everything he has to the regular deal-ers and collectors who routinely buy from him. The only items he should sell on eBay or at the local auctions are items that his regulars do not purchase. In other words, his regular customers end up with all the good stuff; eBay and the local auctions get mostly his junk and the leftovers none of his regular clients want.

For the longest time, there were far more pickers and whole-sale dealers than there are today. The lure of quick money on eBay and online stores with very little associated expense has cut deeply into the pockets of those who used to be referred to as "dealers' dealers."

The primary attraction of being a picker or wholesaler is minimal selling expenses in return for a lower price. Both eBay and online catalogs afford wholesale dealers and pickers minimal selling expenses combined with the advantage of near-retail selling prices. Not surprisingly, many pickers and wholesalers ultimately abandon their core customers.

The highly inflated prices once possible on eBay are rapidly becoming a part of the distant past. These days, eBay has effectively abandoned the antique trade, one of the very cornerstones of its early days. It now appears that eBay makes about 90 percent of its revenues selling cars and trucks, consumer electronics, and brand new merchandise.

One might wonder how much time and effort would need to be devoted to improving service for the antique and collectible trade on eBay? One also might also consider what would be the likely outcome the next time eBay is forced by economic necessity to cut jobs. Will eBay axe the jobs of the part of its business that is responsible for producing some 90 percent of its revenue? Or, will eBay cut the staff, or perhaps even the entire service, of the part of its business responsible for producing less than 10 percent of it?

Becoming a Picker

Now that you know all about the valuable service that pickers provide, you have no doubt decided, if you traffic in antiques, that you want to find one to work for you, or, you may have even decided to become one yourself.

All antique shops have to acquire their merchandise from somewhere, and even though some antique dealers frequent auctions and sales, there are countless others who cannot do it because they either do not have the time, they lack the savoir faire, or perhaps they do not own a truck. Even the dealers who do frequent auctions and sales cannot attend them all. If you are smart, you may even buy an item at the same auction a dealer attends and then turn around and sell that dealer the very item he bid on earlier!

To begin the journey to fame and fortune as an antiques picker, all one needs is a small amount of capital. And it can truly be just a little. You can start with as little as $20 - perhaps even less if you are exceptionally resourceful. Although it helps to have a truck or even a station wagon, it is not imperative.

Even if you only have a compact car, you can confine yourself to dealing in small objects - jewelry, silver, old bottles, lamps, glass, and china. In fact, it is helpful to have a particular specialty and these items lend themselves well to the eBay venue.

If you become knowledgeable in a particular field, you will not only become a better buyer, but antique shop owners will learn to trust you and value your expertise in that particular area. Notice that in that last sentence was an extremely important word - trust. The folks you trade with must trust you. Do not take advantage of anyone ever - for any reason.

One does not need to be an antiques expert to be a good picker, but some basic knowledge is required. Next, go to all the antique shops you can locate within whatever range you can cover. Those in larger towns will generally pay more for finds than will the small town shops - but not always. That is one of the many reasons you simply must look for yourself.

When in an antique shop, take your time and check out the merchandise very carefully. Check to see if they seem to favor any particular items. Note, though, a large quantity of a particular thing may well mean that the dealer purchased badly, getting stuck with difficult-to-sell merchandise. You will determine that later.

Check out the shop's prices and then try to memorize them in the broadest of general terms. Survey the prices, keeping in mind that the owner will usually pay around 50 percent to about 70 percent of her ultimate selling price to purchase an item. You will need to pay, at most, about half of the smaller number in order to realize a decent profit. Not to worry though, it is fairly easy to do. Markups as high as 500 percent are common in this business.

Around this time, you can approach the shop owner and engage her in some pleasant banter. Talk around to determining what she has the best demand for, what kinds of items she has difficulty obtaining, and, most importantly, what sort of merchandise she cannot move at all.

Once you have been doing this a while and have gained a fair idea of how it works and have some available capital, you can buy items whose prices are depressed. If you are really confident, you can buy items which have never been in demand but which you feel will be very soon and hang onto them until the market rises. There is not as much risk to this as you may think, as antiques never become any more plentiful, and therefore, prices are certain to rise eventually. The only question is when? At this juncture in your newfound profession, though, it is probably wise not to dabble in longer-term investments.

Let's now go back to the antique shop where you have been engaging in pleasant conversation with the owner. At a point in the conversation when it feels right, tell her you are a dealer, and that you just may be able to supply her with some of the merchandise she needs. Telling her you are a dealer will very likely also enable you to buy from her at substantially reduced prices. Incidentally, it is possible to purchase an item at one of your shops and then sell it for a profit to another shop.

If the owner seems at all interested, find out what type of merchandise she wants to buy and then tactfully ask her the kind of prices she is willing to pay for those items. Once you have learned this, come up with an excuse to keep talking, as antique dealers have been known to be a bit talkative on fairly small matters, and, unless you have nothing better to do, you can fritter away an astounding amount of time simply by being a polite listener. The moment you can take your leave, jot down all that you have learned or it may get very confusing somewhere around the fourth or fifth stop.

Now we will discuss where to buy antiques and more importantly, how to buy them. The majority of your buys will be from these four sources:

- Auctions
- Private party sales
- Other antique shops
- Individuals not involved in the antiques business.

Three factors contribute to the way a dealer prices merchandise:

- How much was paid for it
- What the dealer knows about it
- Whether the dealer has any particular fondness for it

Clearly, there is no set standard for pricing antiques. As you learn more about the various shops in your area, you will learn their pricing strategies or rules of thumb. Because there is usually little or no communication between shops, and because no one can keep track of the vast quantities of merchandise a competing shop may have, you will occasionally find that Things Remembered Antique Shoppe has a particular item you can pick up for say, $5 and for which Aunt Bea's Emporium will cheerfully pay $10. You buy the item (or trade for it) from the first dealer and then sell it to the other.

Eventually, you are bound to encounter someone who has an item she wants to sell, or someone who has an item that he never considered selling and probably does not realize it is an antique, but you are certain you can turn a nice little profit if you can buy at the right price.

Buying from private individuals can be a touchy matter. Remember to be honest and equitable in your transactions. Do not mislead anyone. Chances are fairly good that the individual you will be buying an item from is your neighbor, and if you have misled that person out of a family treasure, you will have to answer for it eventually. So play it straight.

The main difficulty in purchasing from a private individual is in reaching an agreement on an equitable price. Try not to make the first offer - ask how much she wants for the item. That way, should someone come by after you buy the item and inform the seller the price was not enough, she cannot blame you for not having offered a fair price - it was her price.

Of course, should someone offer you a rare umbrella stand for say, $2, and you are certain that you can get say, $200 for it, you would be well advised to offer the person more for it - and not just $5. Let the other person share in the bounty. You will probably sleep a lot better because of it. This can also help you establish a reputation for honesty and fair dealing which can mean repeat business and referrals to you by your customer.

That type of thing will not happen often, though. With remarkable regularity, people overestimate the worth of a family heirloom. If the asking price is too high, figure out what you should be paying for the item and make an offer. Should they refuse, a little bit of haggling is all right, but do not tell them how small a sum the item is worth. You will only make the person unhappy. Simply tell them you are sorry, but the price you quoted is all you can pay, and just let it go.

One technique, which often works well in buying from a private individual, especially when the thing you want is something that is still in use and which has little or no sentimental value, is often called the "new lamps for old" play. For example, if the thing you want happens to be a rare Leica that someone brought back from the World War II and that no one knows how to use, the owner just might swap the Leica for a new inexpensive digital camera that would be of more use to him. And all parties involved will feel they got the best of the trade.

Of course, the above example is a tad unlikely, and was offered purely for illustrative reasons. A more plausible example may be to swap a brand new stainless steel mixing bowl in return for a lovely piece of early Bennington. Either way, you get the idea.

Private sales often are not worth bothering with; however, they deserve a mention prior to moving on to your primary source, auctions. When owners wish to sell all or most of a house full of items and are reluctant to hold an auction, they will sometimes hold a private sale. Sale managers who are professionals will usually come in, price the items, and run the private sale for a percentage of the revenue. Under such conditions, your chances of finding a decent bargain are next to nil. Nonetheless, there is a chance. If you can arrive at a private sale early enough, and have not much else to do, it may be worth a try. All too many sales managers overprice the merchandise being offered with full blown retail prices. Caveat Emptor (Buyer Beware) applies to when you are selling as well as when you are buying.

Once in a while, someone will attempt a private sale without the advice of professional sales people, and if you are lucky enough to find one of these, your chance of getting something you can sell at a profit is fairly decent. Again, be sure you get there as soon as possible, as you are not the only person trying to score a bargain.

Auctions

Auctions will usually be your very best source of desirable goods. They are also the riskiest and most time consuming. In no other venue is it as easy to waste good money on worthless garbage that you neither want nor need.

There are three main types of auctions: government auctions, household auctions and auction house auctions. A word to the wise, auction house auctions always sound really great, but when the purpose is to make money rather than move items out, the price is usually maxed already.

To find out when and where auctions are held, check the local newspapers in the same areas you plan to cover. Household auctions are typically held on either Saturday or Sunday, and they are usually advertised on a Wednesday. Occasionally, you will find an auction in midweek, and these auctions often hold the greatest potential for decent buys since the crowds are a lot smaller.

There are auctions of various kinds at every level of government: state tax division auctions, used merchandise (desks, police cars, computers), and surplus, seized, and forfeited properties (luxury cars, for example). One great and useful place to start your search is **http://gsaauctions.gov/gsa auctions/aucitsrh/** where you can select a state for information on auctions near you or browse by category. These auctions can be conducted both on and offline and sell everything. Do not mistake them for unofficial advertised "get rich quick" government auctions. These are official auctions that each state holds.

I recently attended one where a large gift store inventory was auctioned off in an attempt to recover taxes owed. I purchased quantities of items - after researching them - for pennies on the dollar.

Deciding which auction to hit will most likely be determined by chance at first. Start by attending auctions by all the various auctioneers in the area. When you get to know the local auctioneers, you will know which of their auctions are most likely to yield the best results.

From trial and error, here is a set of auction rules and techniques. Get in to the auction as early as possible before it is scheduled to begin. Doing so will give you a chance to look over the items at a leisurely pace. Take note of the ones you are interested in and determine the maximum price you will pay for each. Since this is surely the most important consideration related to successful auction buying, it bears repeating.

Determine in advance how much you will pay for a particular item and then stick to it. It is extraordinarily easy to get emotional when bidding and pay too much. Do not make the mistake of bidding on an item you really do not need or want simply because it is cheap. Of course, if it is astoundingly cheap, you can no doubt sell it at a profit - but be careful.

It is not necessary that one be secretive when bidding. The widely held idea that one has to be anonymous and stealthy when bidding is simply not justified. We have found that one of the best spots at an auction is front and center, preferably, as close to the auctioneer as possible. By doing this you can see precisely what is being sold and the auctioneer can see you clearly. If you are

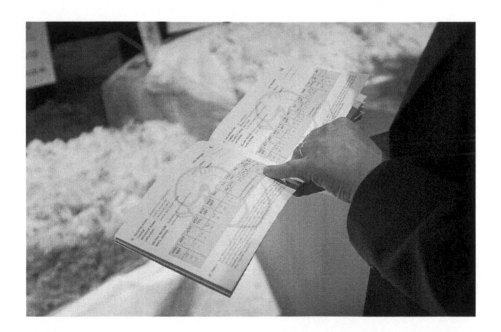

hiding in the background, it can be very easy not to be seen and your bid is missed by the auctioneer.

It is amazing how many people bid on items that they cannot see. Sometimes auctions are swarming with dealers, most of whom miss some good buys simply because they could not see in any kind of detail the items they are bidding on. Any time this happens, you can usually sell your auction purchase at a profit right there at the sale.

It is a very good idea to stay as close to the auctioneer as you can get. Farm auctions are often run right from the front porch of the house. Move right up there by the porch, or better still, on the steps. This provides many advantages besides good visibility. By staying close to the auctioneer, it is easier to make friends with him after just a few sales. Once he gets to know you, he will sometimes abbreviate the bidding on an item that he knows you want, but never ask him to do so. If he does this himself, great; otherwise it is not a good idea.

Positioning yourself up front also provides you the distinct advantage of being able to turn around and face the audience to see exactly who is bidding against you, and they can see you. This advantage is worth the effort.

Auctions really are a game, a satisfying one at that, and if you do not get caught up in the seriousness, they can be wonderful entertainment. Half the fun is in learning to play it well.

A few final notes about auctions: if the bidding appears to be too high, do not waste your time waiting for a decent buy. Sometimes auctions just go this way. There may be more dealers than usual, or for who knows what reason, the bidding is just inordinately inflated. Go find a different auction. Also, hope for rain. It keeps other people away.

If you should have a choice of two auctions, one of which offers a variety of antiques and the other having but a few, it may be a good idea to choose the latter. Odds are most of the antiques dealers and collectors are at the other one.

Old picture frames always do well at auction. However, no one seems to be interested in what is in the frame. It may be a good strategy to let someone else buy the frame. You can often talk them out of whatever is in it, assuming you want it.

At auctions of homes and their contents, there are usually items that will not even fetch the minimum bid, 25 cents. When this occurs, the auctioneer will usually set it aside and move on, adding other no-bid items as he goes. Once in a while, he will bring the whole pile up for a single bid. The pile does not usually bring much because no one wants to tote all that stuff home. But if you are near the  auctioneer, you may see things that may be repairable, or useful. Also, if you buy the junk, you will be a bit further into the good graces of the auctioneer, and you are likely to be able to cull out a few pieces of treasure out of all the trash.

Once you have gone out and purchased a few items, your next move is to sell them to one of your antique shops. If time is not a problem, you may even consider refinishing some of them. Refinishing is not difficult to learn, and a well-done refinishing can significantly increase the value of an item. Many shopkeepers have neither the time nor the inclination to do their own refinishing. Many of those who do that kind of work do not do it very well, and that brings up a brief digression.

If antiques are really your thing, it would be fitting for you to spend some time learning really fine, old-time craftsmanship for repair and refinishing. We are not suggesting you refinish every item just to sell it. In fact, it is probably more important to know when *not* to refinish. Many categories of antiques lose a great deal of value if they are cleaned, renewed, or refinished. Watch a few episodes of Antiques Roadshow on your local PBS channel to see what we mean.

However, if a few hours of light work means you get $50 for a table rather than $5, it is at least worthy of your consideration. If you do decide to learn restoration, learn it well. An extraordinary number of valuable antiques have been destroyed by shoddy work.

If you choose not to refinish, at the very least clean your pieces well before showing them. Simply taking the years of dirt off them can make a significant difference in their appearance and value. Cleaning can be done with just damp rags or Murphy's Oil Soap, but use it sparingly. The idea here is to clean the piece, not strip the finish off. I have used Murphy's to remove 40 years of accumulated tar and nicotine on a dining room set I bought at an estate sale of a deceased smoker. The set was black when I took it home; a week later it was a beautiful rosewood set that we first used and then sold at a substantial profit two years later.

What can you do if you cannot sell an item? Just use it. You can always try to sell it again in just a few weeks or months, as the market changes often. Eventually there will be a buyer for the item. In the meantime, simply enjoy it. This is just one of the perks of being an antique picker. You can furnish your home with antiques and by selling items when the market is good, your decor will never become monotonous. How many others can redecorate with lovely antiques on a regular basis?

At this point, you can consider yourself a true businessperson. Here is a valuable tip for anyone interested in (A) antiques (B) saving money (C) getting a bit of a break on income taxes - which should cover just about everyone. Run right out and get yourself a sales tax license and whatever other licensing might be necessary to operate an antique shop. (It does not cost much.)

When you go into an antique shop, tell them you are a dealer and you will find yourself getting from 20 percent to 60 percent off on whatever you buy. Also, since you are now officially an antique dealer operating a business out of your home, you can legally deduct a percentage (whatever percent of your home is given over to business purposes) of your rent or mortgage payment, automobile expenses (including purchase price if you buy one after you get your business papers), utilities, telephone, as business expenses. If your expenses are more than your income, you can write off a big chunk as a business loss.

Chapter 16

Recommended Items to Offer on eBay

Below are some recommendations for products from successful eBay sellers. Look through it for items that you know about or have a passion for because your feelings will come through in the way you describe your product. One of the best advantages eBay has over the retail store, ironically, is the bond that can develop between seller and buyer because of an understanding or love for a particular product or hobby.

In the days of the general store, a man could lounge, prop his feet up, gossip, and consider the person behind the counter his friend and neighbor. In today's mega stores and fast times, you are lucky to find an associate when you need one and even luckier if the person can answer a question for you. An eBayer can ask any "dumb" question and be reasonably assured of having it answered politely. If you are asked knowledgeable questions about your model train, who knows? You may develop a friendship for life or at least a repeat customer.

These items and categories are in no particular order as you may find your moneymaking niche with anything listed here (and more!).

Selling Information

"Half my lifetime I have earned my living by selling words, and I hope thoughts." — Winston Churchill

The easiest thing to acquire and sell is information. An informational product can be an eBook, a digital report or a white paper, a piece of software, audio or video files, a website, an e-zine, or a newsletter. If you don't want to write, good writers and editors are found right on your computer at **www.elance.com**, **www.journalismjobs.com**, and **www.freelance.com**, for instance.

One lucrative idea is to sell information in form of an eBook: Everyone knows something that others do not and would be willing to pay you some money for providing that information. After you have created an eBook it becomes your exclusive product. You can sell it for the price you feel the information is worth and what people would be willing to pay. You can start your own affiliate program and let other affiliates promote your product for a certain amount of commission.

If it is informational, instructional, or educational in nature, it can be considered an informational product. Why should you create your own informational product?

- There's no inventory to stock
- There are no shipping and handling charges
- It is fast to create, fast to market
- The startup costs are low
- You can automate the sales and delivery process

A manufacturing plant does not have to make your merchandise. You do not have to spend months designing a new product. If you have a computer and a word processor, you have everything you need to create a best-selling information product in a short amount of time.

You do not have to write to create a great info product. If you do not have the ability to create the product yourself, there are several avenues you can take to information product success.

- **Hire a ghost writer** - A ghost writer is someone who will write the eBook for you anonymously, with the writing credits going solely to you. You supply the expertise and guidance and the ghost writer puts it in a readable format. You can hire ghost writers on an hourly basis or for a flat fee, depending on the scope of the project. Or you can become a ghost writer of online information.

- **Co-author with a Writer** - Expert knowledge is much harder to come by than great writing skills. If you are an expert on a subject that people will pay to learn about, you may choose to pay a good writer to take your knowledge and put it in a saleable form. If you are a writer, becoming a co-author means that both of you get credit for creating the product and share in the revenues.

- **Publish a directory** - If you are drawing a blank here, try compiling a directory. A directory is nothing more than a listing of specialized information that you target market to a particular segment of the buying public. It requires no knowledge and no skills. It is usually a listing of company names, addresses, phone numbers, and email and website addresses. Research an industry, compile your list, package it, and sell it online.

As for subjects, here are some ideas:

- **Feel their pain** – Someone in pain wants information on a cure. Do them a favor and provide information on the latest research (which you have researched).

- **Offer advice** - Everyone knows something or has a perspective on something that will open someone else's eyes. If you give advice, make sure it is incontrovertible.

- **Write for the Few** - Make sure you are writing for a highly defined audience. There is more money in giving mothers seven characteristics of a well-adjusted two-year-old than you will get writing about toddlers in general.

- **Entertain Them** - People love drama and humor. Increase the power of your product by adding entertainment that makes them want more. Their interest will fill your pockets.

- **Give Them a Taste** - Give people a sample of what you offer on your website and on eBay in your information product (eBook, for example). Persuade people to buy your information by giving them the first chapter to listen to or read.

- **Pick a Timeless Topic** – Avoid subjects of fad or trends. Create the product once and keep the sales rolling in for years to come.

Books

Finding a genre may be equivalent to finding your niche. A yard seller's collection of books on a particular subject, such as black magic, could spark an eBay bidding frenzy from other collectors.

The constant best eBay sellers among books are not on *The New York Times'* best seller lists. They are textbooks. If you live near a college, or better yet, are in college, this is the way to go. College teachers receive dozens of free books for trial or review to the point of having to get rid of them. Another tack is to advertise for what you want.

Beware of automatically snapping up any first edition book you find as only the occasional first edition is worth anything. Also, avoid book club selections as they are a glut on the market.

EBay and mega stores have not quite put all the small bookstores out of business, but you can bet that the small store owners have the Internet and are looking for something their regular customers like.

Non-fiction sells very well on eBay. Look for books in good condition on subjects such as art, photography, transportation cars, trains, planes, military guns and  aircraft, animals, how-to books, courses, local and regional history, and recent antique price guides. Children's books sell very well if they are in excellent condition and children's pop-up books get snapped up quickly if they are in tip-top condition. Teenage girls' books are hot sellers, particularly if they are hardcover.

In general, however, stay away from cookbooks. There are too many on the market to carve out a niche with them. Use their information, instead, for your own online articles about health, nutrition, and at-home fast food.

Best sources for books are garage sales, flea markets, your local thrift shop, and online.

Software

If you do not know how to create your own software program to sell, you can easily hire a professional to do this job for you. Simply do an online search for software programmers.

Internet Services

Some of the common Internet services are graphics design, Web designing, Web hosting, search engine submission, and search engine optimization. You can choose any of the above options and use it to build an online business and sell the same product on eBay as well.

Anything on Wheels

Autos and accessories now represent the top category on eBay, with the highest gross merchandise volume above every other category. EBay derives 90 percent of its income from vehicles, and more cars are sold on eBay than anywhere else in the world. According to eBay, a vehicle sells on the site every 52 seconds and a part sells every second!

Rewards for selling vehicles would dazzle any seller. EBay auto-related sales will reach $7.1 billion this year, continuing a dramatic rise from $750 million in auto-related sales for eBay in 1998 before it separated those items into the auto-specific area. An SUV sells on the site every six minutes.

Auto sales started on eBay with collectible cars selling side by side with Matchbox cars and other auto-related memorabilia.

According to eBay stats, the most popular cars sold on the site are the Ford Mustang, Chevrolet Camaro, and Chevrolet Corvette.

You can understand how buyers have overcome their distrust of spending large amounts of money with a few key clicks when you realize that General Motors' Saturn's sell well primarily because their prices are not negotiable. People prefer that method of "dealing" over haggling with a used car salesperson, whom is stereotypically distrusted. Buying a used car online means not having to confront anyone face to face, but it also allows a buyer to ask any question without its being fobbed off by a slick dealer. EBay car sellers must be polite, responsive, and honest or quickly lose their entry onto the site.

If you are buying a vehicle or any large purchase online, make sure your seller has a good reputation on eBay. Buy from only those sellers who allow you to cancel the deal after you have seen the vehicle. If you are selling, this is a good sales point to offer.

Cars and SUVs are not alone on eBay. They have been joined by anything that has a motor or wheels: boats, trucks of all sizes, construction equipment, wheel chairs, go-carts, bikes, toy cars, Big Wheels™, and motorcycles. Just name it!

If you wish to enter this market, but in a small way, find a car junk-yard near you where you can buy one good-selling auto accessory or ordinary part— for example, a particular Chevy's tail light cover that you can remove with a screwdriver – and offer it up on eBay. The investment is small, and shipping costs are low. It is a way of dipping your toes in the water or finding your own niche.

The ultimate goal in this category is to become a trading assistant. There is no investment, no risk, and you get a share of the profit in seller's fees.

Collections

Would you believe that keys would sell? A twelve-year old part-ed with his collection of 1,000 keys and opened the door to selling other people's collections on eBay. An artist purchased his keys for use in outdoor artwork she was creating.

If someone has collected it, someone else will buy it. This category is treated in depth in Chapter 4.

Children's Clothing and Goods

Used or new, anything with a well-known label, brand name, designer or boutique name, such as Baby Gap and Old Navy, will find a buyer. A favorite name brand gives the potential buyer another keyword to find your product and make it a best seller. If your children have clothes that do not fit or that they do not want, put the items on eBay. Used children's clothes go quickly because how much wear can a growing child inflict on a dress or shirt? If you are not familiar with the prices of new children's clothing, check them out at Target or even Wal-Mart. Toddler clothing can cost as much as grownup clothing, and they are worn only a few times before being outgrown. Eliminate the items that have stains and group the rest in lots of the same size for boys or girls provide detailed descriptions and such terms as "previously loved" and you are on your way.

You can sell your children's unwanted toys for money you would not have otherwise, or you can scarf them up at yard sales if they are in good condition and worth mailing across the country. That rare old toy that you find may get you a spot on "Antiques Road-show" and some money on eBay.

Old, English China Cups and Saucers

Although it may not be necessary, be willing to shop and sell internationally when searching for china that is out of production. This is just one example of items that collectors on both sides of the Atlantic love, and they are willing to pay well for them. But keep in mind here that just because an item is scarce does not mean that it is desired. The two qualities should run in tandem no matter what you are selling. Extrapolate from this recommendation that you can specialize in one type of antique rather than trying to become an expert in everything made up until 2000. EBay derives the tiniest percentage of its income from antiques, but this is the category where one authentic, special item can bring a huge fortune. Research and luck play a great part in success with antiques.

Vintage Jewelry

Old-fashioned, eye-catching costume jewelry that seems un-usual today may be just the thing to attract a younger, moneyed crowd of buyers. Fashions repeat themselves and you could find yourself on the leading edge with long or fat strands of beads or whopping earrings that are recycling themselves into the current era. It is rare to find a thrift store that has no old jewelry dangling about. Gold is often passed over because it may be too tarnished to glitter. To check whether it is actually gold underneath the brown stains, abrade it gently with a tissue. If the tarnish magically disappears, you have revealed a treasure that is 14 carats or less. Purer gold does not tarnish. This is where your Jeweler's Loupe comes in handy. Look for hallmarks and purity stamps. Read a good book on jewelry to learn what the different numbers used to mark purity mean, or just look it up online.

If you do find a source for gems, semi-precious faceted stones such as amethysts and aquamarines or simple crystals are always in demand, not to mention cabochons of cat's eyes and carved jade. Your buyers may be other collectors, hobbyists, jewelers, or trendsetters.

Media

DVDs sell if you have the very newest releases or older movies on DVD for the first time. Music CDs, cell phones, VHS tapes, rare textbooks, new and nearly new children's books, cameras, printers, printer ink cartridges, cell phones, laptops, disk drives, zip disks, cables, and audio books are what eBay is all about for many people.

Consider also video games, especially PlayStation® and Xbox. Games for the newest systems usually sell best, but hard-to find games from older systems can bring a high price.

Depending on their location, yard sales and thrift stores are the source for older items. Your cost for shipping and supplies are a bargain with USPS. Media Mail saves money, particularly if you mail from your home or office using their pickup service.

Car audio systems are a good niche. Everyone from babies to baby boomers likes having music "to go." Follow the trends through distributors and manufacturers for last year's fad and the newest things on the market. Your merchandise may come from eBay in lots or one by one from a local store or installer.

Dolls

Whether they are expensive collectibles (a $500-R.John Wright's Musette or a $400-Robert Tonner Matt/Sean doll) or just an ordinary baby doll in good condition, there is a buyer. You may be able to buy them on eBay, keep them for a couple of years, and resell them on eBay at a profit. The price for a collectible is not likely to go down. A mint condition doll augmented with blankets, bottles, period costumes, or other accessories will draw the attention of gifters and collectors. Also, people love to buy celebrity dolls (the Marie Osmond Doll, for example), but especially if that celebrity has passed away or is in trouble with the law - strange, but true.

Dollar Store Items

Some people even resell items from a dollar store "as is," but by grouping like dollar items in a giftable container, you may attract buyers who are too busy to run to the store for housewarming or Christmas stocking presents. Small, useless, whimsical, even ridiculous items attract teens and many adults who should know better. Just how necessary, for instance, were those signs in back windows of cars in the '80s that read "Baby on Board" or "Mother-in-Law in Trunk"? Yet, they were everywhere! Someone made a mint.

Anything That Teenagers Like

Why should teenagers not share their generosity with you? Electronic fad items are the way to go here. Just ask any 16-year-old what is in, where to get it, and do your eBay research on recent sales. As with any other fad, you can often quickly determine whether interest is picking up, waning, or possibly recurring and make your move accordingly.

Musical Instruments

Here again, teenagers and children are your friends. Most try an instrument while they are in school and lose interest. You can benefit from their buying and their selling – both done on eBay. You can advertise your need in your local weekly newspaper and start your collection of saxophones, clarinets, and trumpets to auction online. Make friends with your local high school band teachers, as well. They may be able to name your suppliers AND your customers. Check with manufacturers, distributors, and your local instrument shop.

Golf Clubs

Baseball may be America's pastime but the passion is in golf supplies. Here it would help to be a golfer, but eBay can give you a wealth of information on

golf supply sales. If you are not a golfer, invest some time to become knowledgeable about the raging duffer obsession, find your own supply, and develop a niche. To get the basic information, visit a golf store. Golfers love to talk about the "tools" of their game and you only have to listen to learn what they like to own; combine that with your eBay research and then contact a manufacturer or distributor to find out their rules for sharing the wealth with you.

Name Brand and Plus-Size Clothing

Most Americans are overweight and the market has not caught up to their needs that are more likely to be filled online. New or like new name brands are the way to go for all sizes, but your loyal buyers will be those people who are hard to fit. Suppliers are just about any store that sells clothing, any time. The items that are left and marked down at the end of a season, though, are the odd sizes, usually in the high double digits. For your photo, it is amazingly effective to invest in a cheap mannequin that will present clothes far better than your draping it on furniture or hanging it up. Sadly, children are also overweight and there is a shortage of fashionable clothing targeted for them. This is a production as well as a seller's niche waiting for the right person. In this category, it is extremely important to cram your descriptions with keywords to make them pop up on eBay.

Purses and Shoes

There is no such thing as enough. Ask any woman. Styles change every year. Find a wholesale outlet or distributor to be your supplier and run with it. However, "used" will not make you a millionaire in this corner of the market.

Skis, Snowboards, and Camping Gear

Check your local sporting goods stores, wholesale outlets, and eBay for used equipment. There are even collectors of old skis!

Jigsaw puzzles – er – NO!

As an aside here, we would like to recommend one thing you should avoid trying to sell on eBay simply because of the inconvenience. We have heard of people making money with used jigsaw puzzles that they pick up at yard sales and thrift stores, but unless you want to count the pieces to make sure one is not missing, find something else that interests you.

Recommendations from Full-Time eBay Sellers

We asked some people who are earning their living from eBay to give their tips for selling on eBay. Here are their answers.

> *"I sell books, props from movies, coins and art. Unique is great. Ease of handling, storing, and shipping are key."*

> *"I sell Women's fashion jewelry, handbags, clothes, and shoes. I stay on top of the fashion world and industry. This way I'm sure to pick the right products. I do look for uniqueness as this is what really sells well for me. Sizes are important when it comes to clothes. All sizes of clothing sell well, but any lady who sells fashion knows that larger sizes sell best. If you think like a "buyer," you will do great!"*

> *My first question when considering a new product is "Will the product fit into my niche?" Then I ask myself, "Will it sell?" and if so, "Will I be able to achieve my desired profit margin?" The answer to these questions must be "yes" before I will stock the merchandise.*
>
> *I also consider how many of that particular item I can sell. If it will sell slowly, I need to factor that into my decision as well. eBay may seem like a limitless market, but if I have to buy a case of something and I can only sell one or two a month, storage and time cut into the profit margin.*

Just about any item can be shipped or transported to the customer, so I generally do not limit myself to a certain weight or size. If the customer wants to buy it, I want to sell it!

I prefer not to deal with large difficult-to-mail (or ship) items or extremely fragile or highly controversial items that seem to attract problems (such as CDs or couturier brands that may be counterfeit or knock-offs). Therefore, I am middle-of-the-road when it comes to selecting items. I ship mostly USPS Priority Mail, and therefore I select items that can be shipped that way. I met a gentleman at eBay Live (who ships only collectible foreign postage stamps. (If you know the business that is ideal.)

Size and weight are the determining factors in my selection of product. I also look at eBay Hot List, magazines, and commercials to see which products are doing well.

Chapter 17

Building Business Relationships

Get to Know Your Customers

Make a list detailing your customers' likes and dislikes, interests, hobbies, age range, income, occupation, and marital status. Develop a comprehensive dossier on your niche market. The reasons for this will be revealed later as you learn how to create and write an effective sales pitch. It seeks to attract a certain kind of eBay user and is the most effective tool for increasing the sales of your products.

Once you have found your audience, you can stay in touch with them through several different ways. Outside of eBay, you can create blogs, newsletters, and other material that provide useful and informative articles about the subject, and of course, always includes a link to your eBay auctions or eBay store.

Once you have listed more than five or ten auctions, you will then need to employ an effective means of keeping track of them. Simply listing the items, running the auction, and then sending a confirmation email to the winners is inadequate. For example, if a bidder wins one of your auctions and asks whether you have received payment, you need to run down the item by its auction number and see whether you have received the money.

Other customers may wish to know when the auction item was shipped or they may have other questions relating to auctions from the past.

Communicating with Your Customers

Writing Your Descriptions

Before you begin writing, do some competitive research by visiting some other items similar to your own. Note any particularly apt adjectives. Write as though there were no photos. Since a buyer can use only four of the five senses when shopping online, you must compensate with imagery, preferably tailored to your target audience. Without becoming hyperbolic, explain the virtues and benefits of your product or service. Your words link to the reader's imagination. If you know your product, you have a good idea of the sort of person who is reading your description. Therefore, you know the lingo, the style to apply, and whether to be sober, serious, informal, casual, merely factual, joking, or whatever tone the product evokes in its buyers.

Start with an overview of the product. Continue with a more complete description that comes up when the potential buyer clicks the "more details" hyperlink. Be sure to include all the pertinent facts. Try to answer any questions that may arise in the buyers' minds to preclude any delays in the purchase or hesitation on the part of your reader. There is no limit to the length of your description.

Good descriptions can certainly raise your sales above lower priced items. Remember, you may be selling more than just a piece of merchandise. Try appealing to the ego or image of a potential buyer through your descriptions. A little black dress is just a piece of fabric unless you convey that it will make the buyer trendy, enviable, irresistible, desirable, or downright sexy through such wording as "create your own new image" or "add allure to your wardrobe" or "make it a special evening." Check your online thesaurus if you get writer's block.

Be sure to use the words in your description that you would use if you were looking for this particular item. "Keywords" are a word or phrase that people (consumers or businesses) would employ to locate information on the products, services, or topics that they are researching to buy. When choosing your descriptive words, you need to think like a potential customer, not as the seller. You must determine which search terms that a potential customer might use to find your product on eBay.

The description can make the sale, trumping the exact item offered at a lower "Buy It Now" price. In fact, a few days ago, I went online and bought a couple of SmartMedia memory cards for my digital camera. I could have got them for a very cheap price that I found on eBay, but I chose to pay $5 more each for them because the cut-rate description looked cheesy, and I was not sure I could trust them. I was more than happy to pay the extra $10 total when I found the same products at a higher priced site. The description went out of its way to explain its customer service policies to me. I would rather spend an extra $10 and be confident that the cards would show up at my door than lose $30 plus shipping to a site I did not trust.

Your Photos

Few bidders are willing to buy something they cannot see, and few products do not require photos as a selling tool. If your competitor includes an impressive image of his product and you do not, you may lose business.

Including a picture with your eBay auctions is not at all difficult. The basics include a digital camera and the software to run it (Once again, you can also utilize the camera application on your smartphone and simply upload pictures to your computer or email to yourself). EBay has extensive help files on digital imaging. The image should be used to showcase your product. Be sure the lighting and the setup are correct and take the time to take a great picture. When bidders browse through auctions, the image is often the first thing to attract them; therefore, the better the picture, the more bids you will attract.

If you choose to purchase a digital camera, just make sure that it has an adjustable flash (on, off, close-ups, etc.) and will focus down to about 12" or less. This last is very important when shooting small objects like jewelry or taking a picture of a damage or fault in the item.

The Picture Sells!

Another seller's poor photos can mean their failure and your success. Blurry, dark, or tiny photos are doom for a sale. Here are some tips that especially apply for small or intricate items.

- Use plenty of light. If you are taking photos indoors, you should have photo lights (indirect flood lights from various angles) or at least a good flash. You can also use outdoor lighting if you are careful to have an uncluttered background.

- A simple contrasting backdrop will help whether you are indoors or out. For example, when shooting gold or silver jewelry, use a black background. If shooting a darker colored object, use a light or white background. The key here is to experiment until you see what gives you the best quality.

- Get close to your items to eliminate useless space around them.

- Do not put tiny photos in your listing. Minimum recommended size is 600x800 (vertical photos) and 800x600 (horizontal photos).

- Photograph as though there were no description.

- You can use the software that came with the camera to enhance, sharpen, crop and color-correct. But keep your images true to the item…if you are selling a blue dress, don't color correct it so it looks purple.

An important aspect of your eBay auction is an image file for those repeat identical items!

Get to Know Your Suppliers

I have found as a small retailer that there is not a lot of room to negotiate on price, but if I build a relationship with vendors, I can negotiate payment terms. It makes a big difference in my ability to buy inventory to go from COD to Net 30.

Most eBay sellers are small, so we do not have the same negotiating power with distributors that the larger, big box retailers have. My best negotiating tactic is plain old hard work! I get to know my suppliers. I go to trade shows specifically to talk to them in person. I call them on the phone when I have a question. I take the time to talk to my sales representatives if they call or come by. AND I make sure they are paid within the terms of the invoice. These things help build solid personal relationships. In turn, when there is a deal or opportunity, I hope the distributor will think of me.

Another advantage is that my product "line" offers stability of resource.

Conclusion

The Choice Is Up to You

However you choose to build your business, whether it is with limited-life pop culture gear, general manufactured goods, seasonal fun, or valuable antiques, these basics will carry you far.

- Treat your customers well
- Diversify your product line
- Protect your feedback
- Never be afraid to change what is not working for you

Ask for Help

If you go beyond the first step in this book and venture out of your home into your community for items to sell, you may need someone to help. It may be to your benefit to enlist the aid of a family member or friend to help you look, list, and ship. Furthermore most eBay buyers may trust a two-person operation, "Mike&Marie" for example, more than they would, say, "MiketheGuru." Conversely, beware of one-person shops selling on eBay. If there is more than one person at a company selling on eBay, you are far less likely to have problems. A group of people is likely to be more honest than one person may be.

- You may know someone inside an industry who may help you obtain your salable items.

- Perhaps someone you know works in an industry, a store, or likely supplier of your goods. The boss may very well welcome the prospect of not having to deal with returns, or at least, having less work to do concerning them.

- You may want to have someone at the computer as you seek out items. You describe the article on a cell phone, and your helper looks up the information on Google. That way, you will know right away whether you have a gem or not.

No Guts, No Glory

A final thought: use this book as a guide but trust your own good sense and be willing to take a risk.

I used to get Macintosh computers at our local auctions when no one else would touch them. They all wanted PCs, not Macs. Though I knew nothing about them, I knew how to research a part on Google using numbers imprinted on the item, the Mac memory chips, for one. Venturing into a territory - while other auction bidders scoffed - involved doing my own thinking, but it turned out to be very lucrative.

Think of your risks as your investment in yourself. Anyone can follow the crowd; be the one they follow.

Happy selling!

> *"The way to get started is to quit talking and begin doing."*
> -Walt Disney

Merchandise Directory

APPAREL

1 World Wholesale
P.O. Box 1446
Huntington Beach, CA 92647
T: 866-472-7664
International: 714-842-7999
E: CustomerService@1WorldWholesale.com
W: www.1worldwholesale.com
Info: They offer wholesale Sarongs of all types as well as
wholesale clothes, beads, jewelry, art, gifts, and more.

Amor Collections
Kleine Gent 5 B
5261 BS Vught
The Netherlands

T: 073-6565140
M: 06-55-893347
F: 073-6569130
E: amorcollections@home.nl
W: www.amorcollections.nl/en
Info: A wholesale company that imports ladies accessories
    (shawls, slippers, and bags) from India.

Apparel Overstock

Florida and New Jersey
T: 877-9-APPAREL (877-927-7273)
W: www.appareloverstock.com
Info: They offer the lowest prices and best selection on a
    wide variety of wholesale clothing lots including:
    designer labels, urbanwear, children's wholesale clothing,
    men's and women's wholesale clothing, plus sizes, and
    much more.

Ardent Vogue

654 Yonge Street
Toronto, ON
M4Y 2A6
T: 416-907-8605
F: 647-477-2317
E: www.ardentvoguefashion.ca
W: www.aristeyfashion.com
Info: They offer high quality ready-to-wear women's clothes by
    the famous fashion designer Nickolia Morozov.

Aster Shoes Dynamic Sales, Inc.

13070a 91st. Unit 503a
Largo, Florida 33773
T: 727-582-9063
F: 727-587-9528
E: Info@AsterChildrenShoes.com
W: www.asterchildrenshoes.com
Info: They offer high quality children's shoes.

B&A Uniforms

T: 800-741-0322 (Toll-free) or 561-451-0322
F: 561-451-0223

E: unifman1@aol.com
W: www.bauniforms.com

B&W Wholesale
1805 E Highway 304
Pocahontas, AR 72455
T: 870-892-1693
F: 870-892-0812
E: sales@bandwwholesale.com
W: www.bandwwholesale.com
Info: They offer career and casual wear.

babybows.us
2311 60th Street
Brooklyn, NY 11204
T: 718-376-5505
E: designer@babybows.us
W: www.babybows.us
Info: They offer fashion hair accessories for babies, infants
        and toddlers.

Banian Trading
2252 Main Street, Suite #9
Chula Vista, CA 91911-3929
T: 800-366-2660 (Toll-free) or 619-423-9975
F: 619-423-9980
E: info@baniantrading.com
W: www.baniantrading.com

Barr Wholesale Inc.
3350 NW 33rd Street
Pompano Beach, FL 33064
T: 800-831-8337
F: 954-973-9395
E: barr@barrwholesale.com
W: www.barrwholesale.com

Bi-Rite Corp.
111 E. Marquardt Drive
Wheeling, IL 60090
T: 800-437-8773 (Toll-free)

F: 847-808-4155
E: info@bi-rite.com
W: www.bi-rite.com

Blue Moon Button Art
25 Clover Drive
Bayfield, CO 81122
T: 970-884-5256
F: 970-884-5263
E: sales@bluemoonbuttons.com
W: www.bluemoonbuttons.com

Children's Wholesale
10311 Woodberry Road
Tampa, FL 33619
T: 888-755-4888 (Toll-free)
International: 813-661-7785
F: 813-661-7664
W: www.childrenswholesale.com
Info: Monday – Friday, 9am to 6pm Eastern Time

ColorTone
226 NW 4th Ave.
Hallandale, FL 33009
954-455-0200
E: info@ColorTone.com

Comeco
4517 Little John Street
Baldwin Park, CA 91706
T: 800-426-6326
F: 626-813-9140
E: customerservice@comecoinc.com
W: www.comecoinc.com
Info: Wholesaler and manufacturer of handbags, sunglasses,
    belts, and fashion accessories.

Cotton Palace
737 Cortland St.
Perth Amboy, NJ 08861
T: 732-826-2269

F: 732-442-0419
E: sales@cottonpalace.com
W: www.cottonpalace.com
Info: They offer bathrobes for men, women, and children.

Denim Shop Wholesale
4636 Jeanne Street
Virginia Beach, VA 23462
T: (757) 473-1980 or 800-294-8014 (Toll Free US and Canada)
International: 01-757-473-1980
F: 757-473-9989
W: www.denimshop.com

Design Appeal
2301 Stirling Road
Ft. Lauderdale, FL 33312
T: 954-966-7879 or 800-841-3922 (Sales)
F: 954-964-9392
E: michael@designappeal.com
W: www.designappeal.com

Doba.com
1530 North Technology Way
Orem, Utah 84097
T: 877-321-DOBA
E: info@doba.com
W: www.doba.com

Dollaritem.com
2957 E. 46 St.
Los Angeles, CA 90058
T: 323-588-8888 (323-CONCORD)
F: 323-588-8080
E: sales@concordenterprises.com
W: www.dollaritem.com

Brasseur, Inc dba: DonnaVinci
1206 S. Maple Ave. Suite 400
Los Angeles, CA 90015
Tel: 800-320-4193 (Toll Free) or 213-746-2390

F: 213-746-3043
E: info@donnavinci.com
W: www.donnavinci.com
Info: Established 1981; offer high quality women's clothes.

Dorfman Pacific
2615 Boeing Way
Stockton, CA 95206
T: 800-DORFMAN +
   (800-367-3626)
F: 1-800-4DP-HATS (437-4287)
E: custservice@dorfman-pacific.com
W: www.dorfman-pacific.com

Eastern Off-Price Clothing Company
41 Farinella Dr.
East Hanover, NJ 07936
T: 800-526-0793 (Toll-free/US ONLY) or 973-386-1000
F: 973-386-9218
E: customerservice@easternoffprice.com
W: www.easternoffprice.com

Elder Manufacturing Company, Inc.
999 Executive Parkway, Suite 300
St. Louis, MO 63141
T: 314-469-1120
F: 314-469-0523
W: www.elderwearwecare.com

Exotic Silks
1959 Leghorn Street
Mountain View, CA 94043
T: 800-845-7455 (Toll-free)
F: 650-965-0712
E: silks@exoticsilks.com
W: www.exoticsilks.com

Fashion Wholesaler.com
16641 Valley View Ave.
Cerritos, CA 90703
T: 562-404-8557

F: 562-404-0181
E: info@FashionWholesaler.com
W: www.fashionwholesaler.com

Four Seasons General Merchandise
2801 E. Vernon
Los Angeles, CA 90058
T: 877-446-4746
F: 323-582-9630
E: purchasing@4sgm.com
W: www.fourseasonsgm.com

Funky Kids
2284 Canterbury Lane
Wooster, OH 44691
T: 888-773-8659
F: 330-263-5083
E: walia@funky-kids.com
W: www.funky-kids.com

Frisky Shoes
300 Oakwood Lane
Hollywood, FL 33020
T: 954-965-4447
F: 954-965-4443
E: Sales@FriskyShoes.com
W: www.friskyshoes.com

Gametronics
5526 S. Soto
St. Vernon, CA 90058
T: 323-277-3940
F: 323-277-3944
E: info@gametronics.net
W: www.gametronics.net

Gauss Sales Rochester
1555 Emerson St.
Rochester, NY 14606
T: 585-254-3140 or 800-828-6775 (Toll-free)
F: 585-254-3160

E: customer_service@gausssales.com
W: www.gausssales.com

Gaylord Import Sportswear
PO Box 54002
Washington, DC 20032-0202
T: 301 567-8956
F: 301 567-8956
E: gaylordcompany@aol.com
W: www.gaylordcompany.com

Gowholesale.com
T: 877-566-4849
E: sales@gowholesale.com
W: www.gowholesale.com

Hair Utopia dba J & L Company
1633 Kaiser Road NW
Olympia, WA 98502
T: 360-866-8840
F: 360-866-2353
E: sales@hairutopia.com
W: www.hairutopia.com

Hayes Specialties Corporation
1761 East Genesee
Saginaw, MI 48601-2407
T: 800-248-3603
F: 989-755-2341
W: www.ehayes.com
Info: Office hours are from 8:30-5:00 pm EST,
      Monday thru Friday
PP.O. Box 3111

Heart & Soul Sales The Harris Corp.
P.O. Box 3111
Portsmouth, NH 03802
T: 207-363-6773
F: 207-363-6939
E: sales@theharriscorp.net
W: www.theharriscorp.net

Holdup Suspender Company, Inc.
21421 Hilltop St. Suite 16
Southfield, MI 48034-4009
T: 800-700-4515
F: 248-352-1185
E: sales@suspenders.com
W: www.suspenders.com

IDI Carlino, Inc.
1462-62nd Street, Suite 401
Brooklyn ,NY 11219
T: 718-436-9684 or 888-636-9684 (Toll-free)
F: 718-871-4188
E: carlinosocks@aol.com
W: www.carlinosocks.com

Impossible Apparel
12155 Mora Dr. Unit 11
Santa Fe Springs, CA 90670
T: 800-944-8588 (Outside of CA); 562-944-9398
F: 562 941-7889
E: Apparel@impossibleinc.com
W: www.impossibleinc.com

Interbrand LLC
One West 37th Street
New York, NY 10018
T: 212 840-9595 (sales) or 516 349-5888 (customer service)
E: sales.us@interbrandllc.com
W: www.interbrandllc.com

Island Daze
18454 NE 2nd Ave
Miami, FL 33179
T: 305.653.4342
F: 305.653.4341
E: islanddazeusa@gmail.com
W: www.islanddaze.com

Jacobs Trading
13505 Industrial Park Blvd.

Plymouth, MN 55441
T: 763-843-2000
F: 763-843-2101
E: info@jacobstrading.com
W: www.jacobstrading.com

Jazzi Bags
London Branch:
412 Hackney Road
Hackney London E2 7AP
T: 02-076-13-1221
F: 02-077-39-8550
Manchester Branch:
56 Derby Street
Cheetham Hill
Manchester - M8 8HF
T: 01-618-33-3113
F: 01-618-33-3113
E: info@jazzibags.co.uk
W: www.jazzibags.co.uk

John Howard Company, Inc.
4510 Schaefer Ave.
Chino, CA 91710
T: 888-564-6469 (Order Desk—Toll-free) or 909-590-7550
F: 909-590-1346
E: info@johnhowardcompany.com
W: www.johnhowardcompany.com

Jontay
161 Knight Avenue Circle
Waycross, GA 31503-9577
T: 912-287-0401 or 800-783-8925 (Toll-free)
F: 912-287-0449 or 877-673-4448 (Toll-free)
W: www.jontay.com

Julius Young Inc.
38-60 Blanchard Street
Newark, NJ 07105
T: 973-465-7722 or 973-465-7317

E: info@juliusyoung.com
W: www.juliusyoung.com

KN Ltd.
2505 Kerner Blvd.
San Rafael, CA 94901
T: 800-720-0701
E: customerservice@knltd.com
W: www.karenneuburger.com

Kids Resource
200 West Bay Drive
Largo, FL 33770
T: 800-552-1610 (Toll-free in U.S.) or 727-507-8813
F: 727-507-8321
E: kids@kidsresource.com
W: www.kidsresource.com

Killer Beads, Inc.
P.O. Box 18797
Panama City Beach, FL 32417
T: 800-399-7830
F: 850-233-2752
E: sales@knology.net
W: www.killerbeads.com

Kole Imports
24600 South Main Street
Carson, CA 90745
T: 800-874-7766 or 310-834-0004
F: 800-292-1818 or 310-834-0005
E: email@koleimports.com
W: www.koleimports.com

LA Wholesale
1401 South Beach Blvd, Suite #I
LA Habra, CA 90631-1142
T: 866-452-3937 (Toll-free) or 562-902-6420
F: 562-902-6434
E: customerservice@lawholesaledist.com
W: www.lawholesaledist.com

Liloebe LLC
526 West 14th Street, Suite 266
Traverse City, MI 49684
T: 888-440-3013
F: 231-932-9255
E: info@stylease.com
W: www.stylease.com

LITTLE ADVENTURES LLC
40 West 2290 North
Lehi, UT 84043
T: 801-766-8437
E: info@littleadventures.com
W: www.littleadventures.com
Info: Customer Service Hours — Monday-Friday 9:00 a.m. to 4:00
    p.m. MST (excluding Holidays)

LP International
735 Broadway
North Chicago, IL 60064
T: 847-612-5768
F: 847-491-1985
E: info@lpinternational.info
W: www.lpinternational.info

Lowest Priced Clothing LTD
470 Kent Ave
Brooklyn, NY 11211
T: 718-387-3977
F: 718-387-9096
E: Racheloutlets@lowestpricedclothing.com
W: www.lowestpricedclothing.com

Madison Avenue Closeouts
5400 West WT Harris Blvd., Suite K
Charlotte, NC 28269
T: 866-795-7990 (Toll-free)
F: 704-596-0594
E: sales@madisonavenuecloseouts.com
W: www.madisonavenuecloseouts.com

Info: A supplier of off-price wholesale clothing and apparel to retailers, distributors, and online sellers of all sizes.

Main Deal Apparel
1326 S. Main St. #2
Los Angeles, CA 90015
T: 213-749-0379
F: 213-749-0380
E: MainDeal@Pacbell.net
W: maindealapparel.com
Info: A wholesaler specializing in apparel closeouts nationwide.

MegaGoods, Inc.
2741 South Alameda Street
Los Angeles, CA 90058
T: 800-788-7618
F: 323-234-3211
E: cs@megagoods.com
W: www.megagoods.com
Info: An online drop-shipper with a large selection of brand name items at wholesale prices.

Merry-Go-Round
Unit 13, Twyford Mill Estate
Oxford Road,
Adderbury, Oxon. OX17 3SX
United Kingdom
T: 01869 337650
W: merrygorounduk.co.uk
Info: Offers a selection of baby & children's clothes from well-known major brands at factory shop prices.

Simplx Broker Advisor Simplicity Group, LLC
2250 North University Parkway #4894
Provo, UT 84604
E: inquiry@simplx.com
W: www.simplx.com
Info: Dropping Service for over 10 million products

Merchandize Liquidators
430 Ansin Blvd., Suit G

Hallandale, FL 33009
T: 800-218-9596 or 954-454-7100
F: 954-455-7824
W: www.merchandizeliquidators.com
Info: They specialize in wholesale closeouts and liquidation,
    overstock, and surplus from most department stores in
    the USA.

MONAG KIDS
7350 Sachem Trail
VICTOR, NY 14564
T: 585-742-8056
F: 585-302-4475
E: service@monagkids.com
W: www.monagkids.com
Info: An importer and wholesale distributor of children's
    apparel and clothing.

MyLeather.com
955 Venice Blvd.
Los Angeles, CA 90015
T: 800-514-0544
F: 213-741-1134
E: info@myleather.com
W: myleather.com

NAFTA Traders
600 North Wildwood
Irving, TX 75061
T: 972-438-7253
F: 1-972-554-8286
E: Sales@naftatraders.com
W: www.thecloseoutwarehouse.com
Info: A leader in the athletic closeout industry.

NationalGift.com
12550 W. Colfax Ave. #119
Lakewood CO 80215
T: 888-658-8714 x 103
F: 888-658-8714
E: Service@NationalGift.com (For general inquiries)

W: nationalgift.com
Info: Provides wholesale gift baskets, candy, flowers and other
    wholesale products to resell.

Neals Ties
T: 215-914-0459
F: 215-947-8757
E: info@nealsties.com
W: www.nealsties.com
Info: Importer of novelty ties. They sell to retail stores, tie
    distributors, neckwear wholesalers, and flea markets.

New World Sales
207 Union Street
Hackensack NJ 07601
T: 800-237-8901
E: rflorie@newworldsales.com
W: www.newworldsales.com
Info: They represent multiple wholesale manufacturers who
    produce a wide variety of licensed t-shirts, hats, toys,
    stickers, posters, and other items.

NORTH PINES, INC.
814-D West Innes Street
Salisbury, NC 28144
T: 704-637-3456
F: 704-637-5123
E:northpines@CBI1.NET
W: www.northpines.org
Info: A wholesaler of off-price active wear and accessories.

Overstock Hats
1301 Ridge Row
Scranton, PA 18510
T: 800-233-4690
F: 800-882-5428
W: www.overstockhats.com
Info: Wholesalers of closeout hats and overstock hats with
    wholesale bulk purchasing.

Pandamerica Imports, Inc.
1076 Horizon Drive # 1
Fairfield CA 94533
T: 707-422-1280 or 800-637-9889 (Customer order telephone number)
F: 707-422-1397
W: pandamerica.com
Info: They have a large selection of high quality hats, bags, and shoes manufactured in Europe and Asia.

Pontier International
13230 E. Firestone Blvd., Suite K
Santa Fe Springs, CA 90670
T: 562-404-8557
F: 562-404-0181
E: info@PontierUSA.com
W: www.gifts-pontier.com
Info: Manufacturer & Distributor of wholesale handbags, purses, and jewelry.

Premier International, Inc.
34300 Lakeland Rd.
Eastlake, OH 44095
T: 216-426-1513
F: 216-426-1499
E: info@premierinternationalinc.com
W: dollarstoredist.com

Quality Custom Lanyards
5270 South Zinnia Court
Littleton, CO 80127
T: 800-952-0305 (Toll-free) or 303-979-7928
F: 303-979-4901
W: www.qualitycustomlanyards.com
Info: They offer wholesale high quality personalized lanyards.

RHC Wholesale
1790 West 8th Ave.
Hialeah, FL 33010
T: 305-888-1674
F: 305-888-4435

E: info@carlosr.com
W: www.carlosr.com
Info: Wholesale undergarments, socks, pajamas, and more.

RED EARTH CLOTHING Kauai Screen Prints
3116 Hoolako Street
Lihue, Kauai Hawaii 96766
T: 808-245-5123 or 800-799-5834 (Toll-free)
F: (808) 245-8730
E: sales@redearthhawaii.com
W: www.redearthhawaii.com
Info: Hawaiian Clothing Manufacturer of unique and Earth-
friendly apparel for wholesale or retail.

redtagclothing.com
1615 E. 15th Street
Los Angeles, CA 90021
T: 213-744-0400
F: 213-744-1667
E: helpdesk@redtagclothing.com (customer service) / main@
redtagclothing.com (sales)
W: www.redtagclothing.com
Info: Wholesale clothing. Office hours are 9a.m. to 5p.m.,
Monday through Friday (PST).

Safety Technology
1867 Caravan Trail #105
Jacksonville, FL 32216
T: 800-477-1739 or 904-720-2188
F: 904-720-0651
E: info@safetytechnology.com
W: www.safetytechnology.com
Info: Dropship wholesaler of self defense products, hidden
cameras, spy, and surveillance systems.

Saville 1300 Inc.
23795 Lake Drive
Crestline, CA 92325
T: 888-824-9929 (Toll-free) or 909-338-8360
M: 310-291-7732 (24 Hours)
F: 909-338-8370

E: david@saville1300inc.com or sherry@saville1300inc.com
W: www.saville1300inc.com
Info: Authorized wholesale distributor of the full line of
    NuBra® self-adhesive gel bras and related products.

Selini Neckwear
22 West 27th Street 2nd Floor
New York, NY 10001
T: 212-725-7222
F: 212-725-6595
E: help@selinineckwear.com
W: www.selinineckwear.com
Info: Store Hours are Monday through Friday from 8 a.m.
    to 6 p.m. and Saturday from 8 a.m. to 4 p.m.

Shasta Liquidations
P.O. Box 984
Bella Vista, CA 96008-0984
T: 877-293-9293 (Toll-free for customers only) / 530-243-1248 for
non-customers
F: 877-293-9293 (Toll-free)
E: shaliquidations@sbcglobal.net
W: www.wholesalecentral.com/giftex0001/
Info: They offer wholesale items in many popular categories
    including apparel, home décor, hard goods, soft goods,
    stationery, toys, fashion accessories, party items, sports,
    and much more!

SHOENET.com A subsidiary Tradings.net Inc.
1350 Broadway, Suite 1004
New York, NY 10018
T: 212-947-3220
F: 212-683-2163
E: info1@shoenet.com
W: shoenet.com
Info: The first online wholesale shoe store.

Silver Wolf
P.O. Box 405, RPO
Corydon, Winnipeg, MB R3M 3V3 CANADA
T: 204-475-0825

F: 204-452-4441
W: www.silverwolfcanada.com

Smethy Merchandise
Miami, FL 33161
T: 866-904-7713
E: info@smethywholesale.com

Stay Up
1640 Colby Ave #12
Los Angeles, CA 90025
T: 310-473-0775
E: alexdeleon@stayup.com
W: www.stayup.com
Info: A clothing line and online boutique based in Los Angeles
    that has been doing business since 1995 and offers
    wholesale to retailers.

Sunrise Wholesale Merchandise
PO Box 691300
Los Angeles, CA 90069
T: 877-250-5045
F: 800-858-4986
E: sales@sunrisewholesalemerchandise.com
W: www.sunrisewholesalemerchandise.com
Info: Open 10:00 a.m. to 5:00 p.m., PST; Monday through Friday.
    A free wholesale drop shipper of over 2,500 wholesale
    products.

SW Trading
8000 Harwin Dr # 410
Houston, TX 77036
T: 713-334-8377 (Internet customer service & shipping
department)
F: 713-334-9255
E: support@swtrading.net
W: www.swtrading.net
Info: Wholesaler of fashion handbags, jewelry, & accessories.

Thompson Transfer
Bloomington, Illinois

T: 800-397-8018
F: 309-664-6401
E: information@thompsontransfers.com
W: www.thompsontransfers.com
Info: Distributor of over 5,000 heat transfer designs, blank
      t-shirts, transfer machines, and inkjet paper.

T.H.G. Eco Network
P.O. Box 807
Seal Beach, CA 90740
T: 562-799-9550 or 800-775-1969 (orders)
F: 562-594-8778
E: info@threehighguys.com
W: www.threehighguys.com
Info: Allow you to utilize their network of suppliers for your
      Business to shop for eco products thru one service.

Top Ten Wholesale
T: 800-92-TOP10 (800-928-6710)
E: help@TopTenWholesale.com
W: www.toptenwholesale.com
Info: Allows you to list your company for wholesale buyers
      to see.

JP Communications, LLC.
970 Los Vallicitos Blvd, Suite 222-224
San Marcos, CA 92069-1475
W: www.offpricenetwork.com

Toysdropshipper
1907 East 7th Street
Los Angeles, CA 90021
T:
F: 213-614-7973
E: customersupport@toysdropshipper.com
W: www.alibaba.com/showroom
Info: Provides sellers with large selection of toys, novelties, and
      kids electronics at distributor wholesale pricing.

Ujena Swimwear & Fashion Wholesale Department
1931A Old Middlefield Way

Mountain View, CA 94043-2559
T: 800-448-5362
F: 650-938-1004
E: wholesale@ujena.com
W: ujenawholesale.com
Info: A family-owned swimsuit manufacturer for wholesalers.

UNION OUTLET, INC OFF PRICE SPECIALIST
1436 S. Main St. Suite 7&8
Los Angeles, CA 90015
T: 213-748-9603
F: 213-748-9604
E: unionoutlet@aol.com

Urban Denim Company, Inc
1147 Brook Forest Ave
Shorewood, IL 60404
T: 877-336-9681 (Toll-free)
F: 815-230-3592
E: admin@urbandenimcompany.com
W: urbandenimcompany.com
Info: A worldwide distributor of wholesale hip hop clothing,
     urban wear, and designer clothes for men and women.

USellCorp.com
1313 Midway Road
Menasha, WI 54952
T: 800-741-1523
W: www.usellcorp.com
Info: Will build you an ecommerce Web site already loaded
     with wholesale products.

Via Trading Corporation
2750 S Alameda St.
Vernon, CA 90058
T: 877-202-3616 (Toll free)
F: 877-677-5975
E: sales@ViaTrading.com
W: www.viatrading.com

Info: A wide variety of items purchased directly from
    department store distribution centers and other suppliers
    made available to you through wholesale prices.

Wholesale Central.com Sumner Communications, Inc.
24 Stony Hill Road
Bethel, CT 06801-1166
T: 203-748-2050 or 800-999-8281
F: 203-748-5932
E: sales@sumnercom.com
W: www.wholesalecentral.com

Worldwide Brands, Inc.
2250 Lucien Way, STE 250
Maitland, FL 32751
T: 877-637-6774 (Outside the US: 407-464-9333)
E: Info@WorldwideBrands.com
W: www.worldwidebrands.com
Info: Phone support hours are Monday through Friday from 9
    a.m. to 5:30 p.m. Eastern Time.

Zaken Liquidation Club
20700 Plummer
Chatsworth, CA 91311
T: 818-407-1125
W: www.payjusthalf.com

Zazendi Limited
515 Madison Avenue
New York City, NY 10022
T: 212-831-3353 or 212-860-7760
F: 212-423-0125
E: info@Zazendi.com

AS SEEN ON TV

Boswell Trade Center Inc.
105 South Adams Street
Boswell, IN 47921
T: 765-869-5516 (Main Office) or 765-363-0755 (Auctioneer)

E: auction@localline.com
W: www.closeout-auction.com
Info: They hold dealer auctions every Tuesday for their general
    wholesale merchandise.

Glaze Inc.
800 Apgar Dr.
Somerset, NJ 08873
T: 732-377-5004
F: 732-377-5031
E: info@glazeinc.com
W: www.glazeinc.com

Hydro Sport
11301 Olympic Blvd. #503
Los Angeles, CA 90064
T: 310-473-7036
E: hydrosport@hotmail.com
W: www.hydrosport-usa.com
Info: Water bottles for the 21st century.

BABY ITEMS

Aaron Maternity
215 West Main Street
Albemarle NC 28001
T: 704-986-2207
E: donnaburris@aaronmaternity.com
W: aaronmaternity.com
Info: Wholesale maternity items.

Arian Kids
1207 E 14th Street
Los Angeles, CA 90021
T: 213-622-6036
F: 213-622-5680
E: Day2rm@aol.com

Baby Cakes, Inc.
5880 W 59th Ave., Unit C

Arvada, CO 80003
T: 303-431-2750
F: 509-356-9240
E: babycakes_80003@yahoo.com
W: www.babyshowercakes.com

Hold Me and Learn Book-DVD
39311 Diamond Drive
Hemet, CA 92543
T: 951-765-2962 or 877-775-4702 (Toll-free)
F: 951-765-2981
E: heyjow@aol.com

Jay Salez Toys & Baby Products, DVD Accessories
2657 Pacific Park Dr
Whittier, CA 90601
T: 626-456-2141
E: jay@jaysalez.com

JNJ WHOLESALE
6767 Ships Lane
Mechanicsville, VA 23111
T: 804-559-2428
E: customerservice@jnjwholesale.com
W: jnjwholesale.com

Karen's Keepsakes LLC
11 Anthony Avenue
Edison, NJ 08820
T: 800-231-9137 (Toll-free) or 908-753-5756
F: 908-561-3702
E: info@karenskeepsakes.com
W: karenskeepsakes.com
Info: Original product line of baby keepsakes.

My Precious Kid
PO BOX 550
Cornelius, OR 97113
T: 503-693-2832 or 800-381-4577 (Toll-free)
E: kay@mypreciouskid.com
W: www.mypreciouskid.com

Nisway Corp.
320 7th Ave. Suite 260
Brooklyn, NY 11215
T: 866-647-9291
F: 866-647-9291
E: info@nisway.com
W: www.nisway.com
Info: Manufacturer of disposable products.

Prime Wear Inc.
112 West 9th Street,
Los Angeles, CA 90015
T: 213-614-0444
F: 213-614-0550
E: primewear@sbcglobal.net
W:www.primewearinc.com

QCU Unlimited, Inc.
6240-2 Metro Plantation Rd.
Ft. Myers, FL 33966-1200
T: 239-332-2205 or 800-729-2205 (Toll-free)
F: 239-332-2093
E: customerservice@qcu.com
W: www.giftbasketsalesupply.com
Info: Wholesale gift baskets.

Rosemont Wholesale, Inc.
3179 Diablo Avenue
Hayward, CA 94545
T: 510-760-7142 or 800-264-7231 (Toll-free)
F: 510-732-5812
E: tanal@rosemontwholesale.com

Rubii Distributed by Far Tar
519 E. 7th St.
Los Angeles, CA 90014
T: 213-627-2398
F: 213-622-9801
E: sales@rubiiwholesale.com
W: www.rubiiwholesale.com

York Marketing Ltd.
PO Box 7345
York, PA 17404
T: 717-733-0015
F: 717-733-0015
E: sharonabend@worldnet.att.net
W: www.wholesalecentral.com/yorkmarketing/

Wholesale Baby Blanks
8503 E Woodcove Dr Suite 125
Anaheim, CA 92808
T: 800-707-9692 (Toll-free U.S.)
International: 001-714-974-1584
F: 714-974-1833
E: sales@wholesalebabyblanks.com
W: www.wholesalebabyblanks.com

BOOKS

American Book Company
New York Showroom/ Sales Office
230 Fifth Avenue, Suite 700
New York, NY 10001
T: 212-684-4100
F: 212-532-9081
Corporate Office
11130 Kingston Pike, Suite 1-183
Knoxville, TN 37922
T: 865-966-7454
F: 865-675-0557
E: Sales@americanbookco.com or flyer@americanbookco.com
W: www.americanbookco.com
Info: The largest, fastest-growing wholesale distributor of
      promotional, closeout, remainder, and bargain-priced
      books.

CAMERAS

Buy 4 Less Electronics Inc.
2500 Walnut Street, #212
Denver, CO 80205
T: 303-534-7100
F: 303-942-3666
E: sales@buy4lessinc.com
W: www.buy4lessinc.com

Eclipse Distribution Inc.
6835 Shiloh Rd E Suite C-7
Alpharetta, GA 30005
T: 678-947-9147
F: 678-947-9149
E: sales@eclipse-distribution.com
W: www.eclipse-distribution.com
Info: A direct distributor for Mustek, Apex, Coby, Vivitar, Astar, and DXG

JNL Trading
2740 Beverly Dr. Unit C
Aurora, IL 60504
T: 630-779-2455
F: 630-820-8703
E: sales@jnlelectronic.com
W: jnlelectronic.com

COLLECTIBLES

D&L GIFTS AND NOVELTIES
4880 TULSA AVE.
Olivehurst, CA 95961
T: 530-742-1275
F: 530-742-1275
E: giftbringer@prodigy.net
W: www.wholesalehub.com/giftbringers1.html or www.wholesalecentral.com/dnlgif0001/store.cfm

Fine-Line Products Inc.
738 10th Avenue
Grafton, WI 53024
T: 800-558-9850
E: finelinesales@aol.com
W: www.fine-lineproducts.com

G&Z International, Inc.
10923 Indian Trail, Suite #105-107
Dallas, TX 75229
T: 972-488-5550 or 800-881-9488 (Toll-free)
F: 972-488-5591
E: info@gzintlinc.com
W: www.gzintlinc.com

JAC's Wholesale
108 E. Pitt Street
Tarboro, NC 27886
T: 252-823-5510
F: 252-823-5517
E: jacs@wholesalenc.com
W: www.wholesalenc.com

Lasting Impressions International Inc.
330 Tompkins Avenue
Staten Island, NY 10304
T: 718-556-1500
F: 718-556-4074
E: info@lastingimpressionsintl.com
W: www.lastingimpressionsintl.com
Info: A manufacturer and distributor of imported rocks,
      gemstones, and novelty items.

MASCOT INTERNATIONAL INC
1055 Harrison Street
Berkeley, CA 94710
T: 510-527-3965
E: mascotintl@aol.com or mascotintl@sbcglobal.net
W: www.mascotusa.com
Info: A manufacturer and marketer of patented and copyrighted
      giftware since 1974. Includes a unique collection of 24K

gold-plated and chrome-plated items mounted with Austrian crystals.

Wild Ginger Imports
539 Elm St Rte 101A
Milford, NH 03055
T: 877-945-3446 (Toll-free) or 603-673-1574
F: 603-672-7083
E: wildgingerimport@aol.com
W: www.wildgingerimports.com

COMPUTER PRODUCTS

J & S Computing Steve Carter
20 Erford Rd Ste 12
Lemoyne, Pa 17043
T: 717-975-8595
F: 717-909-7020
E: jands@bellatlantic.net
Info: A used computer parts wholesaler.

CRAFTS

Ann' Artome
226, F.I.E., PATPAR GANJ INDUSTRIAL ESTATE, DELHI 110 092, INDIA
T: (+91 11) 22145045 / 22145046 / 22145047
F: (+91 11) 22145048
E: info @ annart.net
W: www.annart.net
Info: Wholesale from India: scarves, stoles, sarongs, bandanas, pareos, jupe skirts, footwear, fashion jewelry, and lots more!

Asian Handicrafts
310, Udyog Vihar, Phase-2
Haryana - 122 016 (India)
T: +(91)-(124)-3014411/3014422

F: +(91)-(124)-3014412
E: asianh@vsnl.com
W: www.asianhandicrafts.com
Info: Manufacturer and exporter of a collection of
      handcrafted items.

INDIAN HANDICRAFT EMPORIUM
5, Main Mehrauli Road (Near Qutab Minar),
New Delhi- 110030 (India)
T: 26514599, 26514577, 26563156, 26563482
F: 91-11-6865405
E: info@treasure-india.com
W: www.treasure-india.com

Kagzi Handmade Paper Industries
Gramodyog Road, Sanganer
Jaipur, Rajasthan- 303 902, India
T: +(91)-(141)-2730019/2730076/3314518
F: +(91)-(141)-2732065/2732065
E : kagzi@datainfosys.net or kagzi_jp1@sancharnet.in
W: www.kagzipaper.com
Info: India based organization presenting themselves as the
      leading manufacturer, exporter, and supplier of handmade
      paper and handmade paper products.

Almar Shell Industries Main Branch Factory
514-A Behind San Isidro Church Talon-Talon 7000
Zamboanga City Philippines
T: (63)(62) 992-1620
F: (63)(62) 991-6123
E: marlyn@almar-shell.com
W: www.almar-shell.com
Info: An export business established in 1982 and presently
      engaged in manufacturing different kinds of shell
      products.

New Era Overseas
C-49, Vivek Vihar, Phase-I
New Delhi - 110 095, Delhi, India
T: +(91)-(11)-22158326 / 55341763
M : +(91)-9818033122

F: +(91)-(11)-22158326
E: newerai@ndf.vsnl.net.in or info@neweraoverseas.com or sales@neweraoverseas.com
W: www.neweraoverseas.com
Info: Manufacturer, supplier, and exporter of eco-friendly
    handmade paper and handmade paper crafts.

Peoplink.org
11112 Midvale Rd
Kensington, MD 20895
T: 301-949-6625
E: peoplink@peoplink.org
W: www.PEOPLink.org
Info: Non-profit marketplace enabling you to purchase directly
    from artisans all over the world.

Sara-P CNX Limited Partnership
56 Soi Wachirathamsatit 10, Sukhumwit 101/1 Road,
Bangna, Bangkok 10260, THAILAND
T: +66 2747 8566
F: +66 2747 8075
E: heritageth@ego.co.th
W: www.heritagethai.com

DOLLAR STORE ITEMS

ABCO INTERNATIONAL
P.O. Box 574125
Orlando, FL 32857-4125
T: 407-896-6000
F: 407-896-5458
E: abco11@juno.com
Info: Variety of costume and sterling silver jewelry.

Accessories Palace Inc.
1953 10th Avenue North
Lake Worth, FL 33461
T: 561-582-1812
F: 561-582-1435

E: order@accessoriespalace.com
W: accessoriespalace.com

DollarStoreSource.com
4425 East 49th Street
Vernon, CA 90058
T: 800-360-9070
F: 800-890-7302
E: contact@yourpremiersource.com
W: DollarStoreSource.com
Info: A full service company providing general merchandise, specialty items, giftware and seasonal items.

GALAXY DISTRIBUTORS
1691 B CHURCH STREET
HOLBROOK, NY 11741
T: 631-563-3990 or 888-281-2789 (Toll-free)
F: 631-563-4066
E: galaxytoys@optonline.net
W: www.wholesalecentral.com/galaxy/store.cfm

The Lingerie Center
2340 Barker Oaks Drive, Suite 400
Houston, TX 77077
T: 281-531-6900 or 800-930-6955 (Toll-free)
W: sales@thelingeriecenter.com
W: www.thelingeriecenter.com
Info: Sellers of name brand and off-price lingerie at 50 to 80 percent off retail prices.

Merchandise Access
P.O. Box 385
Syracuse, IN 46567
T: 574-457-8600 or 877-457-8601 (Toll-free)
F: 574-457-8625
E: merchacc@ligtel.com

World Source Group
14801 S McKinley Ave
Posen, IL 60469
T: 708-272-4447

E: worldsourceinc@sbcglobal.net

Info: A general merchandise wholesaler of everything from health and beauty to dollar store merchandise.

Cyber Acoustics, LLC.
3109 NE 109th Ave
Vancouver, WA 98664
T: 360-883-0333 (Office) or 360-823-4100 (Tech Support)
F: 360-883-4888
E: info@cyberacoustics.com
W: cyberacoustics.com
Info: Hours are Monday through Friday from 8:30 a.m. to 5:00 p.m. Pacific Standard Time (Except Holidays).

7 Elephants Distributing Contact Person: Benny Chen
2965 E. Vernon Ave
Vernon, CA 90058
T: 323-587-8778 Ext: 105
F: 323-587-8998
E: Benny@7elephants.com
W: www.7elephants.com

Worldus, Inc.
175 Lauman Lane
Hicksville, NY 11801
T: 516-933-4902 or 800-853-9310 (Toll free)
F: 516-933-4901
E: sales@worldus.com
Info: Manufacturer, importer, and wholesale distributor of scrap and memory books, photo albums, and accessories.

CANDLES, INCENSE, POTPOURRI

ADEEP NOVELTIES ADEEP INC.
1528 North Main Street
Roxboro, NC 27573
T: 336-599-4705
E: dilip@adeepnovelties.com
W: www.adeepnovelties.com

Bath Bloomers
4214 C Domino Avenue
Charleston, SC 29405
T: 800-478-8141
F: 843-744-4772
E: sales@bath-bloomers.com or customer_service@bath-bloomers.com
W: www.bath-bloomers.com

Candle Enterprises
19974 129th Ave.
Park Rapids, MN 56470 USA
T: 800-422-6353
F: 218-732-1344
W: www.candleenterprises.com

Matt's Incense
35 Enterprise Drive
Bunnell, FL 32110 USA
T: 386-446-3118
E: incense@mattsincense.com
W: www.mattsincense.com

Moon Cloud Creations
P. O. Box 700243
Saint Cloud, FL 34770
T: 407-319-0339

Scentsational Shoppe, Inc.
945 Amsterdam Ave.
New York, NY 10025
T: 212-531-2007 or 888-271-5242 (Toll-free)
F: 212-865-7781
E: ss2004@verizon.net
W: www.scentsationalshoppe.com

The Globe Imports, Inc.
749 South Kirkman Road
Orlando, FL 32811
T: 407-290-0963 or 800-922-7277 (Toll-free)
F: 407-297-7891

E: sales@globeimports.com
W: www.globeimports.com
Info: A wholesaler and importer of giftware, home furnishings,
    and decorative accents.

Tradex USA Corp
146 W 29th St., Suite 3W1
New York, New York 10001
T: 212-594-6333 or 866-594-6333 (Toll-free)
F: 212-594-2717
E: tradex.usa@conversent.net
W: www.tradexusa.net
Info: Manufacturer and distributor of handicrafts and smoking
    accessories.

Uplift Fragrances
36 Lispenard Ave
New Rochelle, NY 10801
T: 914-403-2207

WV Triple Scents
3410 Gunville Ridge Rd.
Leon, WV 25123
T: 304-532-3178
E: robbie@wvtriplescents.com
W: www.merchantcircle.com

DVDs & VIDEOS

Buy Rite DVD
230 Fernwood Avenue
Edison NJ 08837
T: 877-867-3837 (Toll-free) or 732-661-1110
F: 732-661-1020
E: sales@buyritedvd.com
W: www.dropshipsites.com

DVA, Inc.
DVA West / First National Pictures
4111 W. Alameda Avenue, Suite 305
Burbank, CA 91505

T: 888-447-4147 (Toll-free) or 818-848-6111
F: 818-848-3111
Florida Office:
133 Candy Lane
Palm Harbor, FL 34683
T: 800-683-4147 (Toll-free) or 727-447-4147
F: 727-441-3069
E: callie@dva.com or miguel@dva.com
W: www.dva.com
Info: Distribution Video and Audio (DVA) is a family-owned
    and operated business specializing in the entertainment
    industry.

Empire Distributors, Inc.
4445 North Elston Ave.
Chicago, IL 60630
T: 800-585-3176 (Toll-free)
F: 773-685-0756
E: info@adultsexempire.com
W: adultsexempire.com

General Sound Company
2240 W Washington Blvd
Los Angeles, CA 90018
T: 323-735-1515
F: 323-735-1505
E: generalsoundco@cs.com

Hootie's Outlet
3518 Waterfield Rd.
Lakeland, FL 33803
T: 863-370-2429

Mesarina Distributing
3943 Torrence
Hammond, IN 46327
T: 219-218-4431
E: mesarinadistribut@sbcglobal.net

New Wholesale DVDs
PO Box 100491

Milwaukee, WI 53210
T: 888-777-1908
E: Sales@newwholesaledvds.com
W: www.newwholesaledvds.com

ELECTRONICS

Benchmark Media Systems, Inc.
5925 Court Street Road
Syracuse, NY 13206-1707
T: 800-262-4675 (800-BNCHMRK)
F: 315-437-8119
E: sales@benchmarkmedia.com
W: www.benchmarkmedia.com

Bryston
USA
79 COVENTRY STREET, SUITE 5
NEWPORT, VT 05855-2100
T: 802-334-1201
F: 802-334-6658
E: usaser@bryston.ca
Canada
P.O. BOX 2170
677 NEAL DRIVE
PETERBOROUGH, ONTARIO
CANADA
K9J 6X7
T: 705-742-5325
F: 705-742-0882
E: cdnser@bryston.ca
W: www.bryston.ca
Info: Designer and manufacturer of specialty electronics for the professional and consumer audio marketplaces.

Eyre Electronics
2300-B Central Ave.
Boulder, CO 80301
T: 303-442-7300 ext. 233

Fisher Radio Corporation
27 Daleham Street
Staten Island, NY 10308
T: 718-948-7489
E: fisherdoc@aol.com
W: www.fisherdoctor.com

Granite Audio
925 West Baseline Road, Suite 105 - N2
Tempe, AZ 85283
T: 480-829-8374
W: www.graniteaudio.com

Herron Audio
12685 Dorsett Road, #138
Maryland Heights, MO 63043
T: 314-434-5416
E: keith@herronaudio.com
W: www.herronaudio.com

McIntosh Laboratory
2 Chambers Street
Binghamton, NY 13903
T: 800-538-6576 (Toll-free) or 607-723-3512
F: 607-724-0549
E: feedback@mcintoshlabs.com
W: www.mcintoshlabs.com
Info: Hours are 8:30 a.m. to 5:00 p.m. EST, Monday through
    Friday.

MONARCHY AUDIO
380 Swift Ave., #21
South San Francisco, CA 94080
T: 650-873-3055
F: 650-588-0335
E: monarchy@earthlink.net
W: www.monarchyaudio.com

New Century Audio Canary Audio
P.O. Box 6216
Rosemead, CA 91770

T: 626-500-6261
E: sales@canaryaudio.com
W: canaryaudio.com

Roku
399 Sherman Ave., Ste. 12
Palo Alto, CA 94306
T: 1-888-600-7658 (ROKU)
International: +1-650-321-1394 x18
F: 650-321-9648
E: sales@rokulabs.com
W: www.rokulabs.com

Sonos
223 E. De La Guerra
Santa Barbara, CA 93101
T: 805-965-3001
F: 805-965-3010
W: www.sonos.com

FOOD PRODUCTS

ABC Bakery Supplies
7200 N.W. 1st Avenue
Miami, FL 33150
T: 305-757-3885
E: iaaguilar@dsli.com
W: www.abcbakerysupply.com

American Key Food Products LLC
1 Reuten Drive
Closter, NJ 07624
T: 877-263-7539
F: 201-767-9124
E: contactus@akfponline.com
W: www.akfponline.com

BK Enterprises & Worldwide Specialty Foods
6512 Eastwick Avenue
Philadelphia, PA 19142
T: 215-724-4040 or 800-354-9445

F: 215-724-4044
W: www.bkfoods.com

CANELLE - Specialty Foods
5220 NW 72nd Ave # 5
Miami, FL 33166
T: 305-403-3300
F: 305-594-1126
E: info@canellefoods.com
W: www.canellefoods.com

Colossus Int'l Trading, Inc.
136 S. 8TH AVE, STE 1,
LA PUENTE, CA 91746
T: 626-452-9739
F: 626-448-7372
E: info@cittrading.com
W: www.wholesalecentral.com/cit/

DDW Distribution
15480 Aviation Loop Dr.
Brooksville, FL 34604
T: 352-799-1060
F: 352-799-0066
E: sales@ddwonline.com
W: www.DDWonline.com

EVERGREEN MARKETING, INC.
Most items ship from Baltimore, Maryland
T: 410-653-2596 or 800-296-2596 (Toll-free)
F: 410-486-3425
E: f4green@erols.com
W: www.f4green.com

Gourmet Products Inc.
1925 W. Copans Road
Pompano Beach, FL 33064
T: 800-464-0416
E: cs@gourmet-products-inc.com
W: gourmet-products-inc.com

International Foods
200 Main Street
Burlington, VT 05401
T: 802-658-8700
F: 802-658-8787
E: info@oliveimports.com
W: oliveimports.com
Info: Importer and distributor of Greek and Mediterranean
    foods.

National Sales Corp.
6250 S. Boyle Avenue
Vernon, CA 90058
T: 323-586-0200
E: info@e-nsc.com
W: www.e-nsc.com

New Frontier Marketing
701 Seneca Street
Buffalo, NY 14210
T: 716-845-5548
F: 716-845-5456
E: sales@newfrontiermarketing.net
W: www.newfrontiermarketing.net

ROCK BOTTOM DEALS
7101 W. 60TH ST.
CHICAGO, IL 60638
T: 773-229-9780
F: 773-229-9781
E: sales@rockbottomdeals.biz
W: www.rockbottomdeals.biz

Woodland Foods Inc.
2011 Swanson Court
Gurnee, IL 60031
T: 847-625-8600
F: 847-625-5050
E: sales@woodlandfoods.com
W: www.woodlandfoods

GENERAL MERCHANDISE

AmeriSurplus Corporation
240 University Parkway
Aiken, SC 29801
T: 803-643-0606
F: 803-643-0801
E: info@amerisurplus.com
W: www.amerisurplus.com

Brandywine Liquidators
333 Falkenburg Ave, Suite B-204
Tampa, FL 33619
T: 813-413-4415
F: 813-413-4425
E: sales@blinclink.com
W: www.brandywineliquidators.com

Bryco Distributing
Midwest City, OK 73110
T: 866-392-9785
F: 405-610-2272
E: Info@BrycoDistributing.com
Info: Salvage truckloads, store returns, wholesale, pallets, eBay
    supplies, reverse logistics

Closeout Services Corp.
380 Rector Place, Ste 6E
New York, NY 10280
T: 212-945-1765
W: closeoutservices.com

Coastline Industries Inc. Contact: Mel Rollins III
P.O. Box 7
Holly Ridge, NC 28445
Physical Address:
301 Hwy 17 South
Holly Ridge, NC 28445
T: 910-329-4170
F: 910-329-4171
E: surplus@coastlineindustries.com

D.J.H. Inc.
5390 N.W. 161st Street
Miami Lakes, FL 33014-6224
T: 305-620-1990
F: 305-620-1775
E: Sales@DJHINC.com
W: djhinc.com

G.B.Y. Liquidations
14231 Seaway Road B4
Gulfport, MS 39503
T: 228-575-3880
F: 228-575-3882
E: sales@gbyliquidations.com
W: www.gbyliquidations.com

GDC Commodities Exchange
4603 North Brawley #104
Fresno, CA 93722
T: 559-271-3290 or 800-404-9449 (US/CAN)
E: info(at)gdc-ce.com
W: www.gdc-ce.com

Hilco Wholesale, LLC
5 Revere Drive, Suite 206
Northbrook, IL 60062
T: 847-509-1100
F: 847-509-1150
E: mail@hilcowholesale.com
W: www.hilcowholesale.com

Inter American Wholesale Liquidators
300-1 Suite 6 Route 17 South
Lodi, NJ 07644
T: 973-614-0700 or 800-614-0700
F: 973-614-0600
E: contact@iawholesale.com
W: www.iawholesale.com

Jacobs Trading Company
13505 Industrial Park Blvd.

Plymouth, MN 55441
T: 763-843-2000
F: 763-843-2101
E: info@jacobstrading.com
W: www.jacobstrading.com

LiquidationCloseouts.com
T: 212-725-2642
F: 212-725-0132 or 800-456-9492 (Toll-free)
E: sales@liquidationcloseouts.com
W: LiquidationCloseouts.com
Info: Hours are Monday through Friday
      from 9:00 a.m. to 7:00 p.m.

Liquid XS
230 5th Avenue, Suite 912
New York, NY 10001
T: 212-447-1550
F: 212-447-1551
E: memberservices@liquidxs.com
W: www.toydirectory.com/liquidxs.com
Info: Monday-Friday 9am-5pm EST

**Moonlight Entertainment & Sales World Wide Media
Liquidators**
P.O. Box 269
Goodland, KS 67735
T: 785-899-5947
W: www.moonlightsales.com

NAWCA (North American Wholesale Co-Op Association)
P.O. Box 56
Pioneer, OH 43554
Corporate Offices:
1616 E. Roosevelt Road
Wheaton, IL 60187
T: 1-800-537-7849
E: webcontact@nawca.org
W: www.nawca.org
Info: Members can access the web's largest wholesale product
      and supplier database.

Ninostrading.com
Physical Address:
369 Albano Drive
Tonittown, AR 72762
Mailing Address:
PO Box 6820
Springdale, AR 72766
T: 479-361-9998
F: 479-361-9972
E: info@ninostrading.com
W: Ninostrading.com
Info: Business Hours: Monday - Friday: 9am - 4pm (CST)

Pallets Mart
P.O. Box 6721
Los Alamos, NM 87544
T: 800-567-2835
E: sales@palletsmart.com
W: palletsmart.com

Rhinomart Industries
8710 Dice Road
Santa Fe Springs, CA 90670
T: 562-907-9656 or 877-447-4466 (Toll-free)
F: 562-907-9659
W: www.rhinomart.com

Sav-On Closeouts
105 W. Highway M-35, P.O. Box 1356
Gwinn, MI 49841
T: 888-662-1097 (Toll-free) or 906-346-7065
E: csupport@sav-on-closeouts.com
W: www.sav-on-closeouts.com

Surplus One, Inc.
301 W. Central St.
Mt. Prospect, IL 60056
T: 847-253-6800
F: 847-253-6886
E: info@surplus1.com
W: www.surplus1.com

Topper International Liquidators
2601 S.W. 31st Avenue
Pembroke Park, FL 33009
T: 800-867-7371
F: 954-454-6730
E: sales@topper.com
W: www.topperliquidators.com

United Auction LLP 2006
306B Capitol St.
Saddle Brook, NJ 07663-6214
T: 973-253-9100
F: 973-253-9101
E: sales@unitedauctionllp.com
Info: They have specialized in liquidation and closeout
    merchandise from famous department stores, retail chains,
    catalog companies, and mail order businesses for over 25
    years.

Value Supply LLC
4828 Dublin Drive
Cleveland, OH 44133
T: 440-230-0508 or 877-358-4204 (Toll-free)
F: 440-372-5684
E: info@vsmerchandise.com
W: www.vs merchandise.com
Info: Their office hours are 8:30 a.m. to 6:00 p.m. (EST) Monday
    through Friday.

West Coast Surplus
100 Scholz Plaza, Suite #210
Newport Beach, CA 92663
T: 949-642-9206 (Also Fax)
E: contact@westcoastsurplus.com
W: westcoastsurplus.com
Info: They specialize in domestics, toys, electronics, clothing,
    footwear, and sporting goods.

Worldwide Liquidators
108 Madison Street
St. Louis, MO 63102

T: 888-869-1273
F: 314-588-1475
E: info@wwliquidators.com
W: www.wwvirtuallyfree.com/REAL_BIG_LIST

GIFTS

Andes Wholesale Market Service
9190 Harner Rd.
Athens, OH 45701
T: 740-594-0801 or 877-594-5959 (Toll Free Order)
F: 740-594-0901
E: sales@andeswms.com
W: www.andewms.com

ArtByGod, Inc.
60 NE 27 Street
Miami, FL 33137
T: 305-573-3011 or 800-940-4449 (Toll-free)
F: 305-573-9343
E: sales@artbygod.com
W: www.artbygod.com

Beautiful Things.net
7 Margaux Ct.
Woodbury NJ 08096
T: 877-678-4100 (Toll-free)
F: 856-251-1597
E: sales@beautifulthings.net
W: www.beautifulthings.net
Info: A family owned distribution company that specializes in
    moderate to high-end fine reproductions of antique pewter
    photo frames, table top items, and vanity, desk accessories,
    and fashion jewelry.

Boston International
89 October Hill Road
Holliston, MA 01746
T: 508-893-0880
F: 508-893-0881

E: Web@BostonInternational.com
W: bostoninternational.com

The Butler Group, Inc.
230 Spring Street #1212 Americas Mart bldg 2
Atlanta, GA 30303
T: 678-344-1778 or 877-288-5371 (Toll-free)
F: 678-344-7807
E: info@butlergroupgifts.com
W: www.butlergroupgifts.com
Info: Sales organization representing manufacturers and
    importers of home accessories, gifts, and personal
    accessories.

Crystalight at the Crystal Castle
81 Monet Drive Montecollum via Mullumbimby NSW 2482
PO Box 495, Mullumbimby NSW 2482 Australia
T: +61 (0)2 6684 3111
T: +61 (0)2 6684 1196
E: info@crystalight.com.au
W: www.crystalight.com.au
Info: Supplier of Quality Natural Crystals, Healing Crystal
    Jewelry, Crystal Singing Bowls, and Metaphysical gifts.

DROMAR INC.
P.O. BOX 6720
OCEAN ISLE, NC 28469
T: 910-287-5411
F: 910-287-5540
E: customerservice@dromar.com
W: www.dromar.com
Info: A wholesale company that does business in the tourism,
    souvenir, and gift market.

Esco Imports, Inc.
6055 Woodlake Center
San Antonio, TX 78244
T: 210-271-7794 or 800-445-3836 (Toll-free)
F: 210-223-1547
W: www.escoimports.com
Info: A supplier of wholesale toys and wholesale novelties.

G&Z International, Inc.
313 S. San Pedro St., Suite #101
Los Angeles, CA, 90013
T: 213-628-7888
F: 213-617-16871
E: info@gzintlinc.com
W: www.gzintlinc.com
Info: Importers and wholesalers of gift, collectible, oriental
    apparel and accessories, and home decoration items.

Garuda Jewelry and Craft
Canada
226 Warwick Avenue
Burnaby B.C. Canada, V5B 3X4
United States
108-2515 Rainier Avenue South
Seattle, WA 98144
T: 877-450-1687 (Toll-free for Canada and U.S.A) or 604-298-0487
F: 866-450-1687 (Toll-free for Canada and U.S.A) or 604-298-2156
E: info@beautifulstuff.com
W: www.beautifulstuff.com

JDW Distribution
612 N. Eckhoff St.
Orange, CA 92868
T: 800-783-9870
E: jdwdist@aol.com
W: jdwdist.com

J and P Sales
Rt. 1, Box 515
Campbell, MO 63933
T: 573-276-3010
F: 573-276-5494
E: info@jandpsales.com
Info: Distributor of wholesale dolls, gifts, and collectibles.

LeSan's Gifts & Accessories
PO Box 382
Washingtonville, NY 10992
T: 845-642-8301

F: 215-243-8537
E: customerservice@lesans.com

J. Ford Company's Gift Business
P.O. Box 2306
Capistrano Beach, CA 92624
T: 949-240-3333
F: 949-493-2627
E: info@GiftBusiness.com
W: www.merchantcircle.com

Perfect Pillow Ltd
Savvy Lifestyle (Mail Order)
One Lantsbery Drive
Liverton Mines
Cleveland, TS13 4QZ.
England UK
T: + 44 (0)1287 644444 or 0500 566500 (Free UK Only)
F: + 44 (0)1287 644244
E: sales@savvylifestyle.co.uk
W: www.aromarelief.co.uk

QuickSilver Dragon
318 John R. Rd. #228
Troy, MI 48083
T: 248-743-0429
F: 248-743-0431
E: janet@lakotacreations.com
W: www.quicksilverdragon.com

Trippie's
1819 Walcutt Road Suite B
Columbus, OH 43228
T: 614-529-9000 or 866-274-1200 (Toll-free)
F: 614-272-5007
W:www.trippies.com

Waterlyn Pty Ltd
ABN 53 080 326 067
National Headquarters
Unit D7 1 Campbell Parade

Manly Vale NSW 2093 Australia
Postal Address
PO Box W256
Brookvale NSW 2100 Australia
T: 02 9948 4333
M: 0412 218 693
F: 02 9948 4366
E: info@waterlyn.com.au
W: www.waterlyn.com.au
Info: Wholesale supply of greeting cards, gift cards, gift paper, and stationery.

GREETING CARDS

ANGELS GREETING CARDS
T: 520-529-8551 or 800-701-3599 (Toll-free)
F: 520-529-8554
E: angelgreetings4u2002@yahoo.com
W: wholesalecentral.com/greetings/

The Greeting Card Man
8325 Stenton Avenue
J.J. Kelly Building, Suite 2B
Philadelphia, PA 19150
T: 866-604-7365 (Toll-free) or 215-753-1000
F: 215-753-1868
E: info@thegreetingcardman.com
Info: A wholesale, manufacturing, marketing, and distribution company.

Henry Brandt & Company, Inc.
8017 East State Highway 76
Kirbyville, Missouri 65679
T: 417-334-0988
F: 417-334-1002
E: Sales@HenryBrandt.com
W: www.henrybrandt.com

Info: A distributor of closeout merchandise, specializing
in categories of products appropriate for resale in the
discount retail industry.

Legacy Greetings
Street Address
707 William Leigh Dr
Tullytown, PA 19007
Mailing Address
PO Box 2196
Horsham, PA 19044-2196
T: 866-GET-LEGACY
F: 215-677-7119
E: sales@legacygreetings.com
W: www.legacygreetings.com

Majestic Greeting Cards Inc.
6600 High Ridge Rd.
Boynton Beach, FL 33426
T: 561-588-8833
F: 561-588-8725
E: hzipkin@majesticgreetings.com
W: www.majesticgreetings.com
Info: Publisher and manufacturer of discount cards, stationary,
invitations, and more.

Nikki's Cards
P.O. Box 1369
Elkton, MD 21922
T: 410-398-6410 or 800-467-0392 (Toll-free)
F: 410-398-6435
E: nikki@nikkisballoons.com
W: www.nikkiscards.com

Inspirations Unlimited
PO Box 5097
Crestline, CA 92235
T: 909-338-6758 or 800-337-6758 (Toll-free)
F: 909-338-2907
E: inspirations0203@aol.com
W: www.inspirationsunlimited.org

Info: Manufacture and distribute greeting cards that look
handcrafted due to hand calligraphy.

Vash Designs
Sales—Doug Perlstadt
677 Spruce Street
Berkeley, CA 94707
T: 415-921-0663 or 800-576-8274 (Toll-free)
F: 415-276-1756
E: doug@vashdesigns.com
W: http:vashdesign.com
Info: They sell mainstream humor cards and a number of more
risqué cards.

HOLIDAY

Adams Wholesale
4040 2nd Street
Wayne, MI 48184
T: 734-595-1606
F: 734-595-1608
E: uniquedist@aol.com
W: www.adamswholesale.com

Coconutz Home and Garden
7025 County Rd. 46 A Ste 1071 #338
Lake Mary, FL 32746
T: 407-628-2626 or 888-480-2626 (Toll-free)
F: 407-628-2626
E: sari@coconutzhomeandgarden.com

DICKENS, INC.
75 Austin Blvd.
Commack, NY 11725
T: 800-445-4632
F: 631-993-3125
E: support@dcgreetings.com
W: dcgreetings.com

Gifts ETC., Inc
Hudson Mall - Route 440
Jersey City, NJ 07304
T: 201-451-2288
F: 201-451-2200
E: giftsetcdirect@aol.com
W: www.wholesalecentral.com/giftsetc/store.cfm

Ocean State Creations
1044 Mineral Spring Avenue
North Providence, RI 02904
T: 401-728-0490
F: 401-728-8577
E: OSCJewlery@hotmail.com
W: www.oscjewelry.com

TWELVE TIMBERS
P.O. Box 813
Richfield, UT 84701
T: 435-893-0175
E: customercare@twelvetimbers.com
W: www.twelvetimbers.com
Info: Regular business hours are Monday through Friday from
       8:00 a.m. to 5:00 p.m. MST.

VARIETY DISTRIBUTORS
134 Bell Street
West Babylon, NY 11704
T: 800-586-9773 (Toll-free)
F: 877-554-7766
E: howardberko@cs.com
W: www.varietydistributors.com

JEWELRY

Best Imports & Wholesale
4081 Summer Ave.
Memphis, TN 38122
T: 901-327-0766
F: 901-327-7330

E: customerservice@bestimports-wholesale.com
W: www.bestimports-wholesale.com

BING SALES, INC.
1834 Westminster Street
Providence, RI 02909
T: 401-751-6458 or 800-442-2464 (Toll-free)
F: 401-751-0062
E: sales@bingsalesinc.com
W: bingsalesinc.com
Info: Manufacturers wholesale costume jewelry.

CERIWholesale.com
1104 Coiner Court
City of Industry, CA 91748
T: 626-810-3283
F: 626-810-3231
E: Sales@CERIWholesale.com
W: www.ceriwholesale.com
Info: Wholesale handbags, shoes, jewelry, sun glasses, clothing,
    and belts.

DOGGIE UP
1120 St Andrews Dr
Discovery Bay, CA 94514
T: 925-240-8956
E: doggieup@comcast.net

E'arrs Incorporated
1647 A Oakbrook Drive
Gainesville, GA 30507
T: 770 532-3468 or 800-521-1082 (Toll-free)
F: 770-534-6683
E: earrs@aol.com
W: www.wholesalecentral.com/earrs/

Eastern Origins
8721 Santa Monica Blvd. #1500
Los Angeles, CA 90069
T: 310-455-6817
F: 310-356-4947

E: sales@eastern-origins.com
W: www.wholesalecentral.com/eastern_origins
Info: Wholesale different product categories including, but
    not limited to handicrafts, jewelry, apparel, personal care
    products, furniture, home ware.

Emusicalgifts.com
3820 Ohio Ave., Suite 4
St. Charles, IL 60174
T: 877-514-GIFT (4438) (Toll-free)
F: 630-377-5312
E: customerservice@emusicalgifts.com

Fa Fa Design Co.
2424 Poplar Blvd. #A
Alhambra, CA 91801
T: 626-943-8768
F: 626-943-8778
E: tianliu@sbcglobal.net
W: www.california_webbusiness.com/company_fa_fa_design_
co_1098521

Fashion World
3437 Masonic Dr.
Alexandria, LA 71301
T: 318-542-6148 or 866-420-2403 (Toll-free)
F: 225-612-5810
E: info@americasmartshop.com

Grey Eagle Trader
319 Garlington Road
Greenville, SC 29615
T: 864-281-9914
F: 864-281-9915
E: webmaster@greyeagletrader.com
W: www.greyeagletrader.com

Inch Of Gold, Inc.
3975 Investment Lane
West Palm Beach, FL 33404
T: 800-854-3434

F: 561-842-5572
E: ioginc@aol.com
W: www.inchofgold.com

Koda Imports
1122 C Old Chattahoochee Avenue
Atlanta, GA 30318
T: 877-KODA-IMP (877-563-2467)
F: 404-355-0587
E: support@kodaimports.com
W: www.kodaimports.com

S & J Wholesale
629 South Elm Street, #250
Greensbobo, NC 27406
T: 336-271-6755
E: calsan@cox.net
W:www.sandjwholesale.com

TESOROS DE TAXCO, INC.
12426 N. Columbine Drive
Phoenix, AZ 85029
T: 800-433-6588
F: 800-452-7130
E: daisi@worldnet.att.net
W: www.tesorosdetaxco.com
Info: Wholesalers of handcrafted shell jewelry.

Visage Inc.
29 West 30th Street
New York, NY 10001
T: 888-578 3344 or 212-594 7991
F: 212-356-0016
E: Info@visagewatches.com or info@mdfwatches.com
W: www.visagewatches.com
Info: Designs, develops and distributes watches

Wholesale Jewelry And Accessories
9-11 Johnson Street
Bainbridge, NY 13733
T: 888-563-4411

F: 607-967-3027
E: orders@wholesalejewelry.net
W: www.wholesalejewelry.net

LEATHER

AET, Inc.
140 West Ethel Road, Unit H
Piscataway, NJ 08854
T: 732-248-5400 or 888-722-4537 (Toll-free)
F: 732-248-9600
E: sales@aetraders.com
W: www.aetraders.com
Info: Wholesale leather supplier for biker merchandise.

American Top Leather Inc.
3380 Town Point Dr. Suite 340
Kennesaw, GA 30144
T: 866-681-1256 (Toll-free) or 678-797-0030
F: 678-797-0032
E: sales@americantopleather.com
Info: Manufacturing and wholesale of leather apparel for bikers.

besthandbagwholesale
2319 Creekside Cir. North
Irving, TX 75063
T: 866-PURSES -1
F: 972-488-1251
E: support@besthandbagwholesale.com
W: www.besthandbagwholesale.com

Coco's Intimates
3912 N 29th Ave
Hollywood, FL 33020
T: 954-921-7000 or 877-766 BARE (2273) (Toll-free)
F: 954-921-7055
E: classic@cocosintimates.com or classics@cocosintimates.com
W: www.cocosintimates.com
Info: Hours are Monday through Friday, 10 a.m. to 6 p.m.;
     closed on Saturdays (except by appointment only).

Izabel
100 Independence Way
Danvers, MA 01923
T: 978-762-0984
F: 978-762-0984
E: zarehh@yahoo.com

JD Wholesale
2410 Minnis Dr., Suite 120
Haltom City, TX 76117
T: 817-335-2520 or 866-220-7103 (Toll-free)
E: info@jdwholesale.com (questions) or customerservice@
jdwholesale.com (ordering)
W: www.jdwholesale.com

Linda Look Inc.
1600 North Chico Avenue
South El Monte, CA 91733
T: 626-579-3879
F: 626-579-3825
E: info@lindalook.com
W: craftsuppliers.a2zyp.com

Marshalwallet.com
10002 NW 50 St
Sunrise, FL 33351
T: 888-5-Wallet
E: Info@Marshalwallet.com
W: marshalwallet.com

Roma Leathers, Inc.
1180 E. Francis St. Bldg. B
Ontario, CA 91761
T: 909-923-3368 or 800-998-7662 (Toll-free)
F: 909-923-3118
E: thomas@romabags.com or roma@romagunbags.com
W: www.romagunbags.com

S&S Vegas Distributors
P.O. Box 43798
Las Vegas, NV 89116

T: 877-347-5187
E: sales@ssvegasdistributors.com
W: www.ssvegasdistributors.com

Western Express, Inc.
300 Villani Drive
Abele Business Park
Bridgeville, PA 15017
T: 800-245-1380
F: 412-257-5020
E: support@westernexpressinc.com
W: westernexpressinc.com

MUSIC

BEST DEAL MOVIES
2750 Oregon Court Suite M4
Torrance, CA 90503
T: 310-328-5565
F: 310-328-5575
E: Sales@BestDealMovies.com

CD Plus Entertainment/Dolphin Video
5000 Park St. North
St. Petersburg, FL 33709
T: 727-487-3593
F: 727-546-5101
E: Jeremy@cdplusdolphinvideo.com
W: drop[shipblueprint.com/cd¬llus_dolphin_video

HORIZONS MUSIC
122 14th Street
Mendota, IL 61342
T: 815-539-3775
F: 815-539-3776
E: horizons@cdlps.com
W: www.horizonsmusic.com

Sunshine Joy Distributing
P.O. Box 12

Woonsocket, RI 02895
T: 877-769-8800 or 401-769-8800
W: www.sunshinejoy.com

PARTY ITEMS

Axiom International Inc.
1265 Sannon Blvd.
Billings, MT 59101
T: 800-262-0599
F: 406-248-5576
W: www.axiomintl.com

DICKENS, INC.
75 Austin Blvd.
Commack, NY 11725
T: 800-445-4632
F: 631-993-3125
E: support@dcgreetings.com
W: dcgreetings.com

GeoHorizons, Inc.
855 Parr Blvd, W17
Richmond, CA 94801
T: 510-965-6600 or 800-233-2287 (Toll free)
F: 510-524-4848
E: geohorizons@yahoo.com
W: www.wholesalecentral.com/geohorizons

Home Decoration Accessories, LTD.
N 116 W18500 Morse Drive
Germantown, WI 53022
T: 800-827-2772 (Toll-free) or 262-253-6550
F: 262-253-6544
E: sales@hdaltd.com
W: www.hdaltd.com

K & A Party Supply & Flowers
209 Boyd Street
Los Angeles, CA 90013

T: 888-900-7395 (Toll-free) or 213-626-7395
F: 213-626-7394
E: kapartysupply@yahoo.com
W: www.kapartysupply.com

Magic Fuzzle
4521 West Ravenwood Dr.
Chattanooga, TN 37415-2345
T: 800-496-7938
F: 800-496-7938
W: www.magicfuzzle.com

Party Celebration Inc.
PO Box 2161
Lee's Summit, MO 64063
T: 866-48-PARTY (Toll-free) or 816-537-6338
F: 816-537-6629
E: Party_Celebrate@yahoo.com
W: party-celebration.com

Southern Balloon
12217 S.W. 132 CT.
Miami, FL 33186
T: 800-777-5544 or 305-233-3008
F: 305-233-0769
E: custserv@southernballoon.com or
    feedback@southernballoon.com
W: www.southernballoon.com

SELF-DEFENSE & SECURITY

The BrassKnuckles Company
3499 Lansdowne Dr #206
Lexington, KY 40517
T: 888-604-2296 or 888-604-2296 (Toll-free)
F: 888-604-2296
E: order@brassknucklescompany.com
W: BrassKnucklesCompany.com

Digital Watchguard, Inc.
Corporate Headquarters & CCTV Showroom
1812 Merrick Road
Merrick, NY 11566
Warehouse & Pickup Center
1840 Merrick Road
Merrick, NY 11566
T: 516-868-3600 or 866-340-CCTV (2288) (Toll-free)
F: 516-868-3601
E: sales@digitalwatchguard.com
W: www.dwgdistribution.com
Info: Sales telephone hours are Monday through Friday from
      9:00 a.m. to 6:00 p.m. (Eastern Standard Time).

E-SureShotSales
2025 Chicago Ave., Suite A6
Riverside, CA 92507
T: 951-778-0008
E: wholesale@airsoftpoint.com

Global Supplies Inc.
2657 Mercy Drive
Orlando, FL 32808
T: 407-293-8551
E: globalsuppliesinc@gmail.com

Jaguar Imports
7503 Exchange Drive.
Orlando, FL 32809
T: 407-278-5555 or 800-864-0511 (toll-free)
F: 309-403-6966
E: info@jaguarimports.com
W: www.jaguarimports.com

Kenron Marketing Co.
3729 Calhoun Memorial Hwy
Greenville, SC 29611
T: 864-269-2525
F: 360-351-5913
E: sales@kenronmarketing.com
W: www.kenronmarketing.com

Master Cutlery, Inc.
701 Penhorn Ave
Secaucus, NJ 07094
T: 201-271-7600 or 888-271-7229 (Toll-free)
F: 888-271-7228
E: sales@MasterCutlery.com
W: www.mastercutlery.com

Military Outdoor Clothing, Inc.
1917 Stanford Street
Greenville, TX 75401
T: 800-662-6430 or 903-454-1752
F: 903-454-2433
E: kenneth@mocinc.net (Kenneth/ Sales)
W: www.militaryoutdoorclothing.com

Mojo Wholesale
PO BOX 120887
St. Paul, MN 55112
T: 651-204-3924 or 866-386-6656 (Toll-free)
F: 651-204-9961
E: mojowholesale@gmail.com

Panther Trading Company Inc.
3113 Lorena Ave.
Baltimore, MD 21230
T: 866-644-0134 (Toll-free) or 410-644-0135 or 410-644-0134
F: 410-644-0136
E: Sales@PantherWholesale.com
W: pantherwholesale.com

Point Act
122 North 1800 West #4 & 5
Lindon, UT 84042
T: 801-796-1088
F: 801-796-1089
E: email@pointact.com
W: pointact.com
Info: Business hours are from 9:00 a.m. to 6:00 p.m. (Mountain
    Time) Monday through Friday.

Security Plus Omni Corporation
PO Box 3323
Spokane, WA 99220-3323
T: 800-735-1797 (Toll-free) or 509-363-4261
F: 509-363-4265
E: chris@securityplus.ws
W: www.wholesalecentral.com/omni_security.com or www.
    dropshipsites.com/dropship_suppliers/info/security_396/
    security_plus_omni_corporation.html

Titan Wholesale
PO Box 1875
Westerville, OH 43086
T: 614-738-0019
E: arichey123@direcway.com

SPORTING GOODS

Creswell Sock Mills
103 County Rd. 392
Henagar, AL 35978
T: 256-657-3213
F: 256-657-3214
E: Sales@sockmills.com
W: www.sockmills.com

Game Time
10 Stagedoor Road
Fishkill, NY 12524
T: 845-896-0946 or 888-249-9627 (Toll-free)
F: 845-896-0339
E: info@gametimeshop.com
W: gametimeshop.com
Info: Customer care/business hours are from 8 a.m. to 5 p.m.
    (EST) Monday through Friday.

Paradox Fine Watch Co.
935 Broadway
New York, NY 10010
T: 212-254-9851 or 800-847-9851 (Toll-free)

F: 212-777-0805
E: info@gshockwatch.com
W: www.wholesalecentral.com/paradoxfinewatchco

Pax Trading Inc
20895 Currier Road
Walnut, CA 91789
T: 626-376-1788
E: paxtradinginc@yahoo.com
W: www.wholesalecentral.com/paxtradinginc/store.cfm

Wazirabad Cutlery Inc.
P.O. Box 267
Valley Stream, NY 11582
T: 516-561-3689
F: 516-561-3835
E: sales@WazirabadCutlery.com
W: www.WazirabadCutlery.com

WholesaleForEveryone.com
704 East Park Ave
Hainesport, NJ 08036
T: 888-320-1111 or 609-949-7795
F: 800-406-3733 (267-200-0534) Attention Chris
E: printing@airtimeco.com
W: WholesaleForEveryone.com

Zony, Inc.
218 Little Falls Road, Unit # 3
Cedar Grove, NJ 07009
T: 973-571-0555 or 800-630-9669 (Toll-free)
F: 973-239-1677
E: zonyinc@aol.com

TOOLS & HARDWARE

Action Tool Co., Inc.
1959 Tigertail Boulevard
Dania Beach, FL 33004
T: 800-233-0220 (Toll-free) or 954-920-2700

F: 954-920-8780
E: acttool@aol.com

Calypso Wholesale, Inc.
108 N. 4th St.
Calypso, NC 28325
T: 919-658-8470
F: 919-658-5053
E: calypsowholes889@bellsouth.net
W: www.wholesalecentral.com/calypso/

D and R Imports Inc.
1226 Ramsey St.
Fayetteville, NC 28301
T: 910-484-9433 or 800-206-7847 (Toll-free)
F: 910-484-9438
E: dandrimports829@aol.com
W: www.wholesalecentral.com/dandrimports/

Gary's Wholesale, Inc.
1233 P.A.W. West Park Shopping Ctr.
Mansfield, OH 44906
T: 419-529-0930 or 800-861-5192 (Toll-free)
F: 419-529-0937
E: garyswholesale@rrbiznet.com

ND Wholesale
809 Levee Drive - Suite H & I
Manhattan, KS 66502
T: 785-537-8732
F: 785-293-5528
E: efortunes@yahoo.com
W: www.wholesalecentral.com/nd/store.cfm

Rocky National
2828 London Road
Eau Claire, WI 54701
T: 800-705-2040 (Sales)
F: 715-834-9819
E: sales@RockyNational.com
W: www.rockynational.com

o: Hours are Monday through Friday from 9 a.m. to 5 p.m. (CST).

SHARP IMPORT
6726 Dewey Ave
Pennsauken, NJ 08110
T: 877-286-4139 (Toll-free) or 856-382-0631
F: 856-486-1448
E: Sales@Sharpimport.com
W: Sharpimport.com

York Marketing Ltd.
PO Box 7345
York, PA 17404
T: 717-733-0015
F: 717-733-0015
E: sharonabend@worldnet.att.net
W:wholesalecentral.com/yorkmarketing/store.cfm

TOYS & HOBBIES

Bonita Marie International
1975 Swarthmore Ave
Lakewood, NJ 08701
T: 732-363-0212
F: 732-363-7667
E: sales@bonitaintl.com
W: www.bonitamarie-intl.com

DDW Distribution
15480 Aviation Loop Dr.
Brooksville, FL 34604
T: 352-799-1060
F: 352-799-0066
E: sales@ddwonline.com
W www.DDWonline.com

ya Direct LLC
West Larch Rd. Unit G
, CA 95304

T: 209-830-7600
F: 2098307654
E: sales@daryadirect.com
W: www.wholesalecentral.com/daryadirectllc/

ELCO TOY CO
PO BOX 320152
Brooklyn, NY 11232
T: 718-788-2188
F: 718-788-2208
E: BMatza1@aol.com
W: www.bestwholesalestuffedanimals.com

Karen's Keepsakes LLC
11 Anthony Avenue
Edison, NJ 08820
F: 800-231-9137 (Toll-free) or 908-753-5756
F: 908-561-3702
E: info@karenskeepsakes.com
W: www.karenskeepsakes.com

Mee-Sub Enterprise Corp
14049 Orangevale Ave
Corona, CA 92880
T: 951-727-7335
F: 951-727-7336
E: sales@mee-sub.com
W: toydirectory.com/mee

OKK Trading, Inc.
5500 E Olympic Blvd., Suite A
Los Angeles, CA 90022
T: 323-725-8800 or 877-OKK-TOYS (Toll-free)
F: 323-725-8899
E: info@okktoys.com
W: www.okktoys.com

Pyramyd Air
26800 Fargo Avenue, Unit # L
Bedford Heights, OH 44146
T: 888-262-4867

F: 216-896-0896
E: sales@pyramydair.com
W: www.pyramydair.com

Springer's Wholesale Showroom/Warehouse
1276 W. Lancaster Road
Harmony, PA 16037
T: 877-868-2858 (Toll-free) or 724-368-9972
F: 724-368-9962
E: Springerswholesale@earthlink.net

U.S. Marketing Co.
2571 Rte. 212
Woodstock, NY 12498
T: 845-679-7274 or 800-948-0739 (Toll-free)
F: 845-679-4650
E: usmco@verizon.net
W: http://suppliers.com/u¬_s_marketing_co

Index